Dear Kate,

For
GOODNESS'
SAKE

Spread
The
Goodness

Pamela
Koch

For
GOODNESS'
SAKE

An Inspirational Memoir

The Story Behind the Saint James 9/11 Bereavement Support Group

PAMELA KOCH

Archway Publishing books may be ordered through booksellers or by contacting:

Archway Publishing
1663 Liberty Drive
Bloomington, IN 47403
www.archwaypublishing.com
1 (888) 242-5904

ISBN: 978-1-4808-6976-9 (sc)
ISBN: 978-1-4808-6975-2 (hc)
ISBN: 978-1-4808-6977-6 (e)

Library of Congress Control Number: 2018966377

Printed in the United States of America.

Archway Publishing rev. date: 5/14/2019

Through Him, And With Him, And In Him ...
Eucharistic Prayer

Contents

Introduction

Yes, it is true, that in the telling of the story, we are healed. Even seventeen years later as I finish writing this book, the story of 9/11 lives on in infamy, as it forever will. The stories of that day are being shared in homes and in our schools, on sidewalks and in coffeehouses everywhere, at our places of work and worship, at Ground Zero, and in countries all over the world.

Reflecting on the history of our country before 9/11 calls to mind the catastrophic loss of life that resulted from the Pearl Harbor attacks on December 7, 1941. That day is still memorialized in many ways now, some seventy-seven years later. Survivors tell their stories, and citizens visit the Pearl Harbor Memorial. The memories live on through video and print of that horrific day when 2,388 men and women lost their lives. In President Franklin D. Roosevelt's first draft of his speech to the American people after the Pearl Harbor attack, the opening line referred to "A day that will live in world history." Roosevelt changed that line to read "A day that will live in INFAMY." He was right. We shall never forget the malevolent acts against our homeland and the massive loss of precious humanity robbed from us, nor will we forget the personal grief felt by so many.

Almost sixty years after Pearl Harbor, our nation experienced yet another vicious attack resulting in another catastrophic loss of American lives. The 9/11 attacks took place in the largest city in America — New York City — as well as in a field in Shanksville, Pennsylvania, and so close to our nation's capital at the Pentagon in Arlington, Virginia. For those of us living near New York City, this tragic event left a formidable and lasting impact. To know the families affected by this tribulation, to see their faces, to empathize and sympathize with their hearts, and to witness their children experience overwhelming trauma and the traumatic complicated grief that followed is to feel the raw reality of what hatred can accomplish.

In telling my story about The Saint James 9/11 Bereavement Support Group, it is my hope that I can shed a positive light on a community that gave its all in the darkness. It is in becoming the risk takers in life that we can make a difference for another. The people of goodness who bonded together after 9/11 became the catalyst for healing and transformation. It is my belief these people were led by the Spirit of God. It is my hope that other American towns attacked by terrorism may find solace in this story, lending a ray of hope when all hope seems to be lost.

We will not be overcome. We will rise again from the ashes of evil. We will live to tell the story and to answer that familiar question: "Where were you on 9/11?" We will educate our children and pass down the stories to keep 9/11 and our memories of its victims alive. We will work to procure a stronger, more secure, and vigilant nation, striving always to be ambassadors for peace and justice. And so, we will be true to our promise of telling our story to keep alive our memories of the innocent 9/11 victims. The survivor families have made great strides to ensure this outcome.

So too, the illustrious 9/11 Memorial and Museum at Ground Zero, the Freedom Tower, the Oculus, the reflecting ponds at the site along with many creative 9/11 Memorials spread far and wide over this great land will cause all of us to remember and to tell the story.

In the Beginning

A s I reflect on the date of September 11, 2001, I call to mind a book I once read by Charles Dickens that began like this: "It was the best of times; it was the worst of times in this tale of two cities." Although the town we lived in at the time was not a city at all, it was a real, honest-to-goodness, small, suburban American town only thirty-six miles from New York City.

Our town was a safe and abundantly blessed place with many families. Church steeples of many sizes and denominations dotted the small downtown area. The outskirts of town featured open spaces with lovely parks and tree-lined neighborhoods. The town landscape was simple and peaceful with the deer running along the roads and grazing on the lawns of homes. My memory is full of wild turkeys trotting in flocks and horses grazing gracefully down the road from our house. The school system drew families from far and wide. It was a nurturing location to raise a family. Friendly, familiar faces greeted us everywhere we turned. This blissful existence I called home in 2001 was the town of Basking Ridge, New Jersey.

We moved there in the late summer of 1997, and I knew no one other than a few neighbors and acquaintances from the church and school. I commuted to a nearby town where I worked on the staff of a church as a Pastoral Minister. The economy was booming, the housing market was very lucrative, and the tech stocks were out of control.

I thought life was good, and then on December 26, 1997, four months after we moved to Basking Ridge, I was diagnosed with breast cancer — a jolt to anyone's spirit and especially so on the day after Christmas. I spent months on chemotherapy and radiation surrounded by a team of caring people, including not only my family and friends, but also my oncologist and my breast surgeon. For many days, when I was too sick from the chemotherapy to get up, I laid in bed looking out my window remembering the tender, love-filled moments of my life and reflecting on the days gone by. I prayed for courage and the strength to overcome the ramifications of having breast cancer. More than anything else, I wanted to see my youngest son Timothy, who was only nine, grow up. I just loved him and his three siblings so deeply.

As I stared out my bedroom window, memories of my family and my growing-up years flooded my mind. I was born in Bronxville, New York, in Westchester County, on March 12, 1950, to Gabriel and Rita Bundschuh. In my father's early days after college, he worked for the athletic department at his alma mater, Fordham University, and met my mother there she also worked in the athletic office. Fordham University is where it all began. After their courtship, they married and started a family.

Preceding me in the birth order were three older sisters, Maurie, age six, Joan, age five, and Susan, age four. As I arrived into this great big world with many sisters, my father proudly raised the flag and boasted how pleased he was to finally have a harem! My one and only brother, Gabe Jr., appeared a year after me. What joy having a boy brought to the whole family! The flag went up once again! "Bud," as we all call him, truly became "our prince." And then there were six when Noelle Angela arrived home on Christmas morn with a red bow in her hair four years later. Our Christmas angel baby completed our family.

Like many families in the New York City area at the time, we claimed our European heritage with pride. Our mother's maiden name was Murphy, and she was from Irish and English descent. Our father's parents emigrated from Germany. My paternal grandfather had died before I was born, and my paternal grandmother died early in my life when I was about five years old. Even though I was young, I remember her always speaking her native language. I also remember her rimless eyeglasses, her snow-white hair tied up in a bun on the top of her head, and the floral apron she always wore. I remember too, going to a wake in their family home, a ritual that was customary for some Europeans. That wake was my first introduction to death.

Our home was warm and comfortable with a nurturing, loving atmosphere. My dad, Gabe, was an outgoing, friendly person who was greatly loved by everyone who knew him well. A gentle and compassionate man, his warm personality was contagious. He operated a thriving insurance business that allowed our family of eight to live comfortably. He was a patriotic person and a civic-minded individual. He was a person who reached out to help others in the community. Both he and my mother volunteered in the school and for church activities, and, at times, aided both institutions in fundraising.

My mother was an excellent cook. Each Sunday we gathered around the family dining room table to feast on a roast beef dinner. She was creative in many ways and had many friends. She was very ladylike and taught all of her daughters to be the same. For special occasions, she always dressed us in sister dresses, white gloves, and party shoes. Our mother made sure we celebrated our birthdays with fanfare. Holidays, such as Christmas and Easter, and special occasions, like graduations and weddings, were equally festive, and our gifts were always meaningful. The favorite of all was the real live baby chicks at Easter!

Each night before bed, my father prayed "good night" prayers with us when we were young. He also prayed at the dinner table before we ate. I will always remember the words toward the end of his prayer: "May the souls of the faithfully departed through the mercy of God rest in peace. Amen." Through his prayers and conversation, dad, who had six siblings, taught us to remember those who had died in his family, especially his two brothers, my Uncle Pete and Uncle Gerry, as well as his parents.

Since my father's heritage was German, we celebrated various German customs in our home. Every Christmas, my father sang "O Tannenbaum" for us in German. On December 5, the eve of the Feast of Saint Nicholas, we placed our Christmas stockings by the fireplace. The next morning, much to our delight, the stockings were filled with different kinds of fruit.

In keeping with our religious upbringing, all six children in our family attended the parish school, Immaculate Conception in Tuckahoe, New York, for our elementary years. Here I was involved in the Sodality to the Blessed Mother, Brownies, Girl Scouts, and the Catholic Youth Organization in later years.

I spent my high school years at an all-girls school, The Ursuline School in New Rochelle, New York, where my mother, as well as all my sisters, had attended. Among the many experiences, the one that left a lasting impression on me during those high school years was the good feeling that came from helping others. Two moving experiences vividly stand out in my mind. One year, I joined the Thanksgiving food drive and helped to collect and deliver baskets to poverty-stricken areas in the Bronx. After walking into the dreary apartment buildings and going up the dark, graffiti-ridden stairways into the homes of the recipients, it was the priceless, grateful expressions on the faces of the families as we placed our gifts into their hands that touched me so profoundly. This experience and simple act would stay in my heart on my journey through life. Another lasting memory from The Ursuline School was being trained in Confraternity of Christian Doctrine (CCD) or, in other words, as a religious education teacher. Once a week, my classmate Patrice and I would leave school and travel to Blessed Sacrament School on the other side of New Rochelle to teach a religion class for young students. I loved the work and continued it through my college years and well into my adult life. When time moved on from those nurturing and educational days at Ursuline, I took the spirit of outreach to others with me after graduation.

I attended Elizabeth Seton College in Yonkers, New York, where I earned an A.A.S. degree in Retailing. After graduation, I landed a position on Fifth Avenue in New York City as an assistant buyer for a national clothing chain. More eye-opening experiences and growth happened here in the "real world" of the Big Apple, in N.YC.

During my growing-up years, whenever I had free time, I provided childcare for families in my neighborhood. One family that stands out in my mind is the Alfredo family. Frank and Dolores lived several blocks away, from where I lived, with their five beautiful children, each one of them a delight to know. I started babysitting for them when I was eleven years old and they had two children. I continued as their babysitter well into my adult years. Dolores had plenty of cousins nearby, and, when I was in my late teens, she suggested I seek out anyone with the last name of "Koch" at the school social gatherings. Sure enough, I met her cousin Bob Koch at a local Iona Prep graduation party, and two weeks later he asked me out on a date.

Bob and I dated all summer long, and in the fall, he left for South Bend, Indiana, to pursue a degree in engineering at the University of Notre Dame. After writing a slew of letters, continually dating, and taking several trips to Homecoming and football games at Notre Dame, we both knew that the old saying — absence makes the heart grow fonder — was so true. South Bend was far away, and four years is a long time. We made the best of our time that we had together, especially the summer months, which were always the time I looked forward to the most. Summer became like waiting for Christmas to arrive! We planned outings to the beach, picnics, concerts, dinners out, and always a Broadway show. Even though we both worked a lot of the time, we spent any free time together and shared our daily routines.

Bob's projects at the construction company where he worked were challenging and interesting, and we often discussed his day-to-day activities on the job site. His short-term job in the summer months of 1970, between his junior and senior years at Notre Dame, was working on the construction of the World Trade Center in downtown New York City. One evening after picking me up from work, Bob asked if I would like to go with him the following Saturday to the job site and ride to the top of the World Trade Center. What an intriguing invitation! I daresay that not many women had a boyfriend who would take them to the very top of what was the world's tallest building at the time.

The trip to the city was incredible that Saturday! Once we arrived at the construction site, we were outfitted in protective garb: a hard hat, safety glasses, and a reflective vest. We then approached a freight elevator, which was nothing like our modern elevators. This was a wooden box. Now here's where I started to get a little nervous. I stepped into the freight elevator, squeezed my eyes shut, and held on tightly as our wooden box ascended to the 110th floor.

As the doors opened, the site took my breath away! White billowing clouds spread out like a carpet below us. Off in the distance, the spire of the Empire State Building protruded through the billowy white clouds. The sun shone brilliantly above us, and the blue sky left a line of demarcation between the clouds. That was a day I would never forget.

In June 1971, after four long years, Bob graduated from the University of Notre Dame with his degree in Civil Engineering, becoming the first of ten children in his family to earn a degree in engineering. Two of his brothers would follow in his footsteps in years to come.

Not long after Bob's graduation, he invited me to the Auto Pub under the GM building on Fifth Avenue in New York City. We were seated in an old-fashioned car in the "Lover's Lane" section of the restaurant when Bob pulled out a little black box and asked me to marry him. Of course, I eagerly said, "Yes!" Being so very much excited, I showed our waitress my hand with the new sparkling round diamond on it. She congratulated us and asked, "Did this all happen between the salad and the sangria?"

Over dinner, Bob told me how he had made an appointment with my father at his office earlier that day to ask for my hand in marriage. My father, who was overcome with joy for us, took Bob out to celebrate and vowed not to say a word. He did ask if he could share the good news with my mother, and Bob agreed. Shortly after that day, both of our families joined together for brunch at the Windows of The World restaurant on top of the World Trade Center to give a toast to the future bride and groom.

Our wedding day, April 15, 1972, dawned as a rainy spring day. Adorned in my mother's white satin wedding gown and holding a large bouquet of fragrant white roses in full bloom, I entered the majestic sanctuary at the Immaculate Conception Church in Tuckahoe, New York, at noon. Strains of "Jesu, Joy of Man's Desiring" and "Canon in D" played as my bridesmaids in their simple pink long dresses preceded me down the aisle. My sister Joan was my maid of honor. Jennifer Alfredo, our five-year-old flower girl, in her pink frilly dress, spread petals of roses before my entrance. As I took my dad's arm and walked slowly down the aisle, I smiled at our dear family and friends who honored us with their presence. I was delighted to see my CCD class who had been invited to attend the church ceremony. A family friend, Monsignor John Sullivan, officiated the ceremony.

A reception of almost 180 guests followed at the Orienta Beach and Tennis Club in Mamaroneck, New York, overlooking the Long Island Sound. This familiar place is where my family had spent our summers from the time I was five years old. Here, I learned how to swim and was a member of the swimming team. Many good memories were made at the club, and our wedding day was the ultimate memory with no exception. It was a day like no other, and the prize was Bob, my soul mate for life!

How blessed I was when I met this gentle, kind, sensitive, and loving person. Bob was hardworking, and I surmised that he could very well become successful in his chosen field, as it seemed to be a passion for him. We both shared a fascination for his work in heavy construction, and I was sure we would have a lot to talk about across the dinner table in years to come. I also predicted that he would excel on the golf course, which he has. Bob has proven to be a devoted spouse every step of the way. I felt like I was the luckiest girl in the whole wide world ever!

During the early years of our marriage, Bob worked for the Karl Koch Erecting Company, and I worked for Peck & Peck, a clothing retailer, in their buying office. Two years after our wedding, I left my job on Fifth Avenue to start raising our family. We welcomed our first little girl, Kerryn, followed by her sister, Jessica, a Valentine's Day baby. These two little girls became the light of our lives, and many times I could be heard saying, "How did we ever live without them"?

Pink was always on my mind when I entered Sealfons children's department in Ridgewood, New Jersey. My little girls dressed in the lookalike sister dresses with bows in their hair, white tights, and patent leather shoes. I took every opportunity to show them off wherever we went. Their birthday parties were magical with themes like My Dolly and Me, The Teddy Bears Birthday, The Storybook Birthday, The Tea Party Birthday, or The Raggedy Ann Birthday lunch with many heart-shaped cookies and cakes to celebrate. I loved being a mom! These were such happy, happy years making memories and surrounded by family and lots of love.

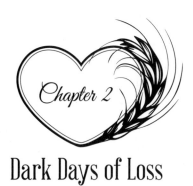

Dark Days of Loss

During those early years of motherhood, I imagined our girls' memories filling up to overflowing with time spent with their grandparents, aunts, uncles, and cousins. The birthday parties, holiday celebrations, graduations, and weddings all swirled with family time. Of course, our family was delighted when my older sister Joan announced her engagement to Donald DeVita, who had recently returned home from his tour of duty in Vietnam. We had a wedding to plan!

On September 20, 1975, my father had the honor yet again of escorting another lovely bride down the aisle. He had had lots of practice and was becoming a pro at it! Joan, who was thirty years old, was marrying the man of her dreams. Our family was filled with happiness and joy on that sunny fall day. None of us imagined the darkness that would envelop our family just over a year later.

On November 12, 1976, my father, the man who had walked four brides down the aisle, died suddenly at age sixty-eight as a result of complications due to heart disease. His sudden death left our entire family numb and in shock.

Dad's funeral mass was standing room only with people packed inside the church and standing down the aisles. As our family proceeded out the doors of the church after the mass, I saw women, as well as men, crying. My father was well thought of by the church, where, ever since I could remember, he attended daily mass. He was an exemplary person and wealthy in friendships, and his honest and trustworthy manner reflected who he was and how he raised his family. He had lived a fruitful life filled with love for his family and friends. We would all miss him terribly.

My father's legacy would continue, of that I was sure. I treasured my memories of him and vowed to hand them down to my children and grandchildren. I will never forget the sight of my father coming through the front door of our family home each night, hugging and kissing my mom like there was no tomorrow, and calling out "Pammielamb" and wrapping me in his warm embrace. I will also never forget the scent of the gardenia corsages he gave all six of his girls (my mother included) every Easter morning. The memories were overflowing, and I was grief-stricken. My children drew me swiftly back into life, as the hectic days of nurturing young children had to go forward.

My older sister Joan was immeasurably comforting to me following dad's death. She was someone I admired and looked up to, and she supported me through every major milestone in my life. Joan and Don arrived at the hospital before anyone else to welcome baby Kerry into the world. When Jesse arrived on February 14, Joan's, birthday, coincidentally, was on the next day, February 15. Whenever Joan had a day off, she would spend time with my girls and me in New Jersey. She was a great help with the children, and I looked forward to her visits.

A beautiful person inside and out with a caring heart and full of kindness and compassion describes our Joan. It was only right that she was called to the profession of nursing. Prior to her marriage, she graduated from Hunter College School of Nursing in New York City and secured a job at Lenox Hill Hospital, also in New York City. I knew her patients were lucky to have her by their sides. Soon after their wedding, Joan and Don bought a charming home in Mahopac, New York, and she continued her nursing at Phelps Memorial Hospital in Sleepy Hollow, New York.

During the first summer that they lived in Mahopac, Joan invited us to a picnic at her lovely home. She had that special touch that made an ordinary day memorable. On this particular day, she spread an array of mouth-watering homemade goodies on the table. We sat overlooking her beautiful garden that she obviously put so much time and effort into. She and Don planned games for the kids with prizes for the winners. Our girls simply adored her and Uncle Don. Later before we left, Joan helped me bathe Kerry and Jesse and put them into their pajamas. We all had a wonderful time visiting and making memories.

And then, as if our family as we knew it had not been rocked enough, Joan was diagnosed with ovarian cancer just shy of her second wedding anniversary. She fought the disease and experienced arduous chemotherapy treatments that caused her to lose her hair and become very ill. I entered a state of denial, believing nothing could ever happen to our Joan. She was so young and so beautiful, with a lifetime ahead of her, truly a woman of promise. No, no, I thought, her death could never happen. And then, exactly six months after Joan's diagnosis, on a cold and damp Sunday morning, March 5, 1978, surrounded by our family at Lenox Hill Hospital in New York City where her nursing career had begun, cancer took my beloved sister's life at the age thirty-three.

Joan's death was too painful. Our dear father had passed away about sixteen months earlier, and now my sister? The grief was overwhelming once again. The word "bereavement" is derived from the Germanic root word, *ber-au-ben*, meaning having been robbed, and that is exactly how I felt — robbed. I remember thinking, "How could this all be happening to us? Why, God, why?"

My maternal grandparents, who had spent a lot of time with us and were very close to us, had died only a couple of years prior to my father and Joan. So, within a five-year period, our family lost four significant loved ones. We were left in compounded grief and filled with overwhelming emotions for a long time. My deep faith and belief system, as well as the support of family and friends, carried me through the grief process.

I did not know it then, but the tragedy, injustice, and deep sorrow that I felt at the time would become the catalyst for leading my life on a journey toward growth and transformation. What I did know, however, was that these loved ones whom I had lost would be carved into my heart and would be with me wherever life took me. The deaths of my father and Joan left a lasting impression on my life, and these life experiences would become the purpose behind my actions in the years ahead.

In 1979, about a year after Joan had died and after the birth of our third child, Robbie, my husband Bob received an assignment for a new project on Cape Cod, Massachusetts. As the engineer, he would coordinate and supervise the renovation projects of the Bourne and Sagamore Bridges over the Cape Cod Canal. Bob and I had never been to Cape Cod, so this would be a new and interesting adventure for our family with three young children, including a four-month-old baby.

When Bob told me we were going to live near the town of Buzzards Bay in Bourne, I felt like crying, and so I did. Our family had been through so much tragedy and grief, and now I was leaving my mother and siblings and Bob's family — my support system. I was teary eyed all the way up to New England. Once we arrived, however, I was heartened by the nautical aura. Soon after we moved, the Corp of Engineers and the ironworkers showed us the spirit of New England's hospitality, welcoming us with open arms at a lively party given in our honor at a popular seafood restaurant near our new project, the Bourne Bridge. While the shadows of grief and the pain of moving followed me, each day became better and better on this new journey in life.

About a year after we moved, Bob received a call at work from his sister Cora. She told him that his twenty-seven-year-old brother, Peter, had been critically injured in a car accident while driving to work on the beltway in Washington, DC. Peter had been a member of the Irish Christian Brothers located at Iona College in New Rochelle, New York. He had been on leave from the Brotherhood, working at a hospital doing a summer program in the Washington, DC, area. Bob left the kids and me on the Cape to join his family at the Virginia hospital where Peter lay on life support. When Bob arrived at the hospital, his parents were in a private room talking with the Organ Donor Team. It was during that meeting that the heartbreaking decision was made to take Peter off life support and donate his organs. This was a very difficult day indeed. Death had entered our lives tragically once more.

Just two weeks earlier, Peter had visited us in Bourne. After learning the sad news of his death, I sat down on our living room couch with my small children cuddled up on my lap. With tears running down my cheeks, I shared the difficult news of Uncle Peter's death with my little ones. I told them that it was okay to cry because someone we loved so much had died. They wanted to know what happened to Uncle Peter, so I explained that he was in a bad car accident, hurt his head, his body could no longer work, and he died. They wanted to know what the words "to die" meant. I explained that Uncle Peter's heart stopped beating and he was not alive like we were. I also added that he was not in any pain.

I told my girls that Uncle Peter's visit was a special gift to us, one that we should always remember. I then encouraged them to remember the good times we had spent with him over the years. I reminded them about what we did when Peter, who was also Jesse's godfather, had visited us, and the places we had gone with him.

"Remember," I said, "we went to Monument Beach and also to one of our other favorite beaches, Old Silver Beach?"

"Yes," they both chimed in. (Robbie was too young at the time to participate.)

"Remember when we ate with him in the train car restaurant near Old Silver Beach," Kerry said excitedly, "And we went to the Cape Cod Mall in Hyannis where we dressed up in the old-fashioned clothes and got our pictures taken?"

Suddenly Jesse piped up, "I remember the bike ride down by the Cape Cod Canal near Daddy's office under the big Bourne Bridge where we went on a picnic with Uncle Peter, and lobster races on the front lawn of our house, and then they turned red when you cooked them, and we ate them for dinner!"

"I remember too," I said, " you told Uncle Peter about the whale with the polka-dotted tail, the mouse in our house, and the bear that combed his hair!"

Yes, we had shared a lot of great memories with Uncle Peter on his visit to Bourne. I spoke lovingly of Peter, how he was a good person and did good things for others, and how he was a teacher and was liked and respected by the young students he had worked with.

The children were most inquisitive of what had happened to Uncle Peter and wanted to know where he was now. I told them that car accidents happen, so we must be very careful when driving in a car and always sit in our car seats and wear our seatbelts. I also told them what we believe, as Christians, that Uncle Peter was with God in a place called heaven. My answer led to a whole new set of questions. I began to recognize this was a teaching moment as I continued to answer their questions honestly on their developmental level.

We prayed for Peter and our family together. I taught them to form a prayer chain, entwining their tiny little sweet fingers with mine, and linking our hands together as we prayed. I helped them use their words along with mine. I then told them it might be nice to draw a picture that I could bring to the wake. More questions came forth from their little mouths and age-appropriate responses from mine.

I taught my children about the word "death" that had entered their young lives on that sad day. It is a word no mother really wants to ever have to teach her children at such tender young ages of one, three, and five. All I truly wanted to do was to protect them from the word for a long as I could. I tried to remain calm, and it was a very grim day. Those precious faces and little beings brought spurts of light into my life as the day moved forward, but then again, they did that every day. I cherished being their mother. In the days that followed, I held them a little tighter and kissed them a little longer.

Living on Cape Cod was a soothing and inspiring place to grieve. We took long walks on the beautiful serene beaches, looking out on the placid blue-green waters of the Nantucket Sound and Cape Cod Bay. These walks were reminiscent of days gone by when Bob and I, while dating, would walk with a young Peter, have picnics, and jump in the waves together at Jones Beach on Long Island, New York. Cape Cod's peaceful atmosphere became a source of healing for our family.

We would continually carry Peter's memory in our hearts in the days ahead.

For the three years that we lived in Massachusetts, our lives were filled with good memories and great relationships that we would always remember. Our girls made many friends at school and we had playdates during the week. We took full advantage of teaching the children what New England was noted for and its history. One Thanksgiving, while the turkey was baking in the oven, we took our visiting family members to Plymouth, Massachusetts, to see the Mayflower and the Plymouth Plantation. (The children and I had read a book earlier in the week on the history of the First Thanksgiving.) We had a great day. In later days we visited the lighthouses of Cape Cod. The children were especially mesmerized when we took them to Provincetown for a whale-watching boat ride.

During our third year in Massachusetts, our children were older, so we planned a weekend vacation trip to Nantucket to see the Whaling Museum. It was so adventurous riding on the ferry over to the island and watching the seagulls following us off the back of the vessel. Once there, the children had fun swimming at the lighthouse beach, and we enjoyed walks through the boat docks. Ice cream cones and trips to the penny candy store were the treats of the day as we wandered along past the many shops on the cobblestone streets of this quaint little whaling village. Here we saw the big boats and ate a delicious fish and chips dinner overlooking the water. Another day we would remember was a trip to Martha's Vineyard for a picnic on our bikes. This was a little bit more of a challenge, to say the least!

I enjoyed teaching religious education, and I was asked to train the First Communion class at Saint John The Evangelist Church in Pocasset, Massachusetts. I worked with great personalities and met my dear friend Chris Perrault who I still stay connected with today.

Living on the Cape was such a blissful experience for our young family that we struggled to leave when the bridge project was completed and Bob was transferred back to our home in Ridgewood, New Jersey. Living in bustling and industrious New Jersey was definitely a faster pace of living than on the Cape. In July 1982, when the moving van pulled away from the front door of our house, tears stung my eyes as we left that tranquil place where our family bonded together so closely, building memories of a lifetime and vowing to return.

Hospice and Bereavement Calling

By 1984, we had sold our home in Ridgewood, New Jersey, and moved to the town of Chatham, New Jersey, which was closer to Bob's main office. Chatham was a wonderful place to raise a family. For the next sixteen years, our family would thrive and make many lasting friendships in Chatham.

Not long after our move to Chatham, I began praying for direction in my life and questioned if hospice work was the right path for me. This was a program that had come into our country about ten years prior into our health field. Ever since Joan had passed away, I wondered, in the back of my mind, whether hospice work would be a way to honor her name. I knew my sister Joan had been visited in her hospital room by hospice workers. She had shared with me the concept of hospice and palliative care for the terminally ill. I wondered how families who were not as large as ours made it through difficult times such as what we experienced. How could I help make it better for others going through long-term illness and loss?

One day, after dropping my son's forgotten lunch off at the Saint Patrick School, I stopped by the church chapel to visit and pray about my idea. I told God I really did not know where to go or who to see about becoming a hospice worker and questioned if I could even do that type of work. Since we were new to the community, I didn't even know the name of the nearest hospital. I told God I would talk to

Him about this at another time, and thanked Him for the goodness in my life. I blessed myself and stood up to leave the church. Just then a woman across from me got up to leave the chapel as well. She introduced herself as Kathy and told me she was praying for her mother, who was dying.

Then, much to my amazement, Kathy told me that what was really helping her at the time was her working for hospice! I explained that I was praying across from her about becoming a hospice volunteer. She told me that Overlook Hospital in Summit, New Jersey was starting its Hospice Volunteer Training Program the following week, and she suggested I call a lady named Margaret. I looked at my encounter with Kathy as an answer to my prayers uttered minutes before. Being truly open to the idea, but somewhat unsure, I went home and nervously dialed the phone number Kathy had given me. I then made the decision to become the risk taker and to enter the training program of this sacred ground of hospice.

After the training concluded, I was assigned patients. I followed my patients weekly, and then, when the illness progressed, my visits became closer together. After the loss of the patient, I followed the families in bereavement for a twelve-month period with notes, cards, and friendly visits. I would encourage the families to seek out the support group at the hospital. I once attended the group with one of the families and saw that the group provided great solace for those who participated.

My pastor at this time was Father Jack Carroll at Saint Patrick Church in Chatham. He was a happy, charismatic, and compassionate man who served the people well. It was an inspiration to share Pastoral Ministry with Father Carroll, as well as with his associate priest, Father Paddy O'Donovan. They both were extremely gifted in ministering to the sick, the dying, and the bereaved. They empowered and enabled me to grow tremendously in ministry work and became mentors for me over the many years we worked together.

Father Carroll had a vision that he shared with me to begin a bereavement support group for the families at Saint Patrick Church going through the death of a loved one. One Sunday after mass, he asked me if I would consider taking a trip for training for the group to the National Catholic Ministry to the Bereaved Conference at Our Lady of The Snows Shrine in Belleville, Illinois. He said the trip would be paid for by the church, and also mentioned I would be joining a friend in the parish whom I knew. I told him I would talk it over with my husband and get back to him.

After I told Bob about Father Carroll's invitation, he encouraged me to go if I wished. I became the risk taker once again and decided to tell Father Carroll that I accepted his invitation. He then took me into his office and handed me a book and some materials to get started in my new role.

The other parishioner attending the training with me was my dear friend, Elaine Mulholland. She was a faith-filled woman who was the mother of five daughters. One of her little girls sadly had died at a very young age, and she had three other beautiful daughters who were stricken with cystic fibrosis. Two of her girls died from the disease prior to our starting the bereavement support group, and the third daughter would succumb to the disease during the time we worked together. Elaine was an inspiration and made my life richer and my faith deeper.

Our training weekend was beneficial and only boosted our enthusiasm for the support group work we were about to begin. We were full of ideas when we returned! By 1986, our support group was thriving. People came from Elizabeth, Jersey City, and West Orange, New Jersey, and even as far away as Connecticut.

Elaine and I became closely connected working with the people. We organized and planned six sessions in the fall and in the spring. We held our meetings in a house owned by the church and located adjacent to the church. Elaine was deeply spiritual and calming for the people. I admired her for the gifts of compassion and love for the bereaved. It was very astute of Father Carroll for teaming us up.

Several years later after the death of her fourth daughter, Elaine retired to Long Beach Island, a place where she had the happiest memories with her girls. I visited with her there several times. I must mention that Elaine had the most glorious voice and was a member of our church choir. Some of her most precious gifts were the beautiful songs that she wrote to her children who died. I learned from her how her musical talent was an outlet to transformative grief and an aid to others at the same time. She showed me more than anything else that a mother filled with such great loss could stand up and step forward once again into life armed with a fervent faith and trust in God who gave her hope and a resiliency to heal others. She was an inspiration to many grieving parents who lost children. Sometimes I wondered if I could ever be so strong walking in her shoes. I truly doubted myself. In 1997 my sweet and beautiful friend Elaine died of cancer. I will always treasure the memory of her with love. Her loss inspired me even more to continue our mission that we had begun.

A year before Elaine's death, the pastors at our church changed, and the new priest, coincidently, came from the same town where I had been born. He was progressive and brought a new model and meaning to our collaborative pastoral staff. Monsignor Ronald Amandolare encouraged me to grow deeper still in my spiritual life as well as in ministry work. Under his leadership, I extended my work into funeral liturgy planning, something I had never imagined or believed I would ever do in my lifetime. I found myself developing a team of compassionate people in the parish to aid families experiencing a death of a loved one and to help make funeral liturgy more meaningful. Along with this effort, I started a support group for the divorced and separated.

I continued to build the Saint Patrick Bereavement Support Group by forming a team of people who wanted to stay within the group. After a year of participating, I gave them the opportunity to train to become a part of our team. Some members did come back for training, enabling the group to build and grow.

Wanting to increase my knowledge in the field, I started obtaining certifications for my enrichment. Since I was a mother of four young children by this time, going back to school was close to impossible, so certifications became my avenue for education. After each conference,

I returned to the group with more ideas. The church supported me, as did my husband, who in many ways helped me to partake in conferences and training weekends.

I became a member of the Association for Death Education and Counseling (ADEC), an outstanding organization that has grown tremendously over the years. Some of my training was through the New England Center for Loss and Transition; the National Catholic Ministry to the Bereaved; and the Saint Paul Center for Pastoral Bereavement Counseling in Staten Island, New York, where I received my certification. I had also received several certifications including "Rainbows" and "Windows" for Children and Teens in Grief and Trauma among several other small workshops I attended. I had many resources at my fingertips as the Saint Patrick Bereavement Support Group moved forward.

An Avalanche of Love

In the late summer of 1997, our family moved from Chatham to a town ten miles west called Basking Ridge, New Jersey. Bob had become president of his company, Koch/Skanska, a builder of steel and heavy construction. Here in Basking Ridge, I received my diagnosis of breast cancer on the day after Christmas. That diagnosis sent me into a traumatic, dark time. I would flash back to the young women whom I had cared for in hospice work. I thought, too, of my sister Joan and the fear we all must have felt while dealing with the similar life-threatening illness of cancer.

My breast cancer diagnosis caused me such sadness, and the pain was only amplified in the rippling aftereffects. I named my losses on paper and at the top of my list was: 1) loss of health, 2) putting our family in a painful situation, and 3) the loss of living my passion to help others.

My passion was the ministry work I shared in. I loved the work — it had become a way of life, a part of who I was. Now it was time to let go and to rethink the life ahead of me, however long that would be. For thirteen years, I had worked at Saint Patrick Church in Chatham. I served the people of the parish and had become a Pastoral Associate ministering to the sick, dying, and bereaved. Among my many tasks, I coordinated bereavement groups supporting adults, young children, and teens, as well as the divorced and separated. I was not only hospice trained, but also trained and certified as a "BUDDY" for AIDS patients, an intense training program indeed.

My treatment took so much out of me. I became forgetful and confused at times. My care team explained to me that chemo-brain was a real side effect of the drug protocol. At times I would trip and fall, another side effect. I attempted to go back to Saint Patrick Church to work, but it swiftly became clear that it just was not the time.

Since I was on the other side of the proverbial coin now, and was the one being cared for, I felt like all of those years where I had helped others were flooding back into my life a hundredfold.

My friends were unbelievable in caring for me. A dear friend and therapist Sister Catherine made visits to my home weekly. At Bishop Jane Methodist Church in Basking Ridge, Diane Garrison, a member of this local church, where I had trained parishioners to minister to the bereaved, called me each week seeking the needs I had for prayer. Diane would then take my wishes back to the community to pray. This community was a group of faithful parishioners who stood by me every week. I recalled being invited once to preach at their Sunday Service and remember vividly this community's warm embrace. My beautiful friend and counselor, Bredeen McGlynn, also visited my home, worked with me on guided imagery, and wrote beautiful poetry for me. My close friend, Kathy Gsell, also a breast cancer patient, came and cooked one of her delicious ginger recipes and continued to stay close to me every step of the way.

My friend, Heidi arrived with her Reiki table. My nurse friends, Nancy, Karen, and Virginia, were around to give me shots, advice, and aid as I needed. My friend Barbara came and treated me to reflexology. Terry brought me funny movies. Parishioners from Saint Patrick Church and families from hospice and the bereavement group came with dinners, soups, goodies, books, angel figurines, and more. Dr. Moriarty visited several times, telling me he just happened to be in the area, to see how my day was going. He is an amazing and compassionate friend.

One day, as my dear friend, Ann Flinn, was shaving my hair off, an entourage of cars showed up at my house. Friends came down my driveway in droves. They came with a delicious garden lunch — "A Taste of Chatham" as they called it — with fine fare from stores around the town. They brought everything I would need to grow a garden: flower and vegetable seeds, gloves, a hat, an apron, shovels, and rakes. It was such an amazing day!

Monsignor Capik brought me communion and a feeling of solace. Sister Cynthia, the principal of Oak Knoll School, brought gifts and sat and had tea. Father Paddy came for a friendly visit with Cathy Gilrane. To this day twenty years later, the Saint Ann Church Samaritan's Group from Parsippany, New Jersey, where I had lectured, shower me with good wishes and many cards on every holiday. Fran Boccella and Pat McNamee took me for chemo treatments.

The list could go on and on. Endless expressions of love and goodness surrounded our family, and they left us sincerely and deeply grateful in our hearts. These many kind acts will always be remembered. I know that these displays of love and affection contributed to my healing in a large way.

Even though I spent many difficult days battling cancer, life continued to march on around me. After I plateaued, regained a good bit of my strength, and received the okay from my doctors to go forward, Bob sent me on a trip with my daughters Kerry and Jesse for a few weeks to Italy, Paris, and Ireland. We found a hint of love and laughter in the air along with the Irish Mist in Ireland when we joined up with my daughters' darling lads, Barry and Bill. My dear friend, Cathy Gilrane, hosted us royally in Westport. It was a grand time for all, with wonderful lasting memories of the green fields, Croagh Patrick, and the beautiful country of Ireland.

A few months later after our return, the new millennium dawned, and Kerry, who was now a nurse, announced her engagement to Barry. Then Jesse and Bill announced theirs, too, only a few weeks later! Both wedding dates ended up being six months apart, so I dove headfirst into planning two weddings.

By this time, Jesse, was pursuing her master's degree. Rob was in his final semester of college, and he planned to work for his father until his full-time financial position started. My youngest son, Tim, was now a thriving middle school student. Life was returning to normal, and I had regained my positive outlook on life that had faded away in the aftermath of my cancer diagnosis.

Late in the summer of 2001 after Rob's graduation and both weddings, I underwent a seven-hour prophylactic mastectomy and reconstruction surgery, performed at Memorial Sloan Kettering Cancer Center in Manhattan. This surgery marked my second one since diagnosis, and six months of the reconstruction process would follow this surgery.

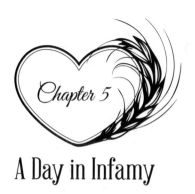

A Day in Infamy

Tuesday, September 11, 2001, dawned as a sunny, crisp morning without a cloud in the blue sky over New Jersey. It was the kind of day that evoked the words "Isn't it the most beautiful day?" I attended to the day's chores, including making breakfast for Tim, who was now thirteen. Other mothers in the homes along Ridgeview Drive were doing the same and preparing to walk our children to the bus stop for a 7:40 a.m. pick up. As Tim and I went out the door, the dew on the green grass glistened in the sunlight.

After seeing Tim off, I returned home to clear the dishes, make beds, and get ready for the day. Suddenly I heard a NEWS ALERT coming from the television in my bedroom. I could hear a news anchor urgently reporting that at 8:46 a.m. a plane had hit the World Trade Center's North Tower. I stopped everything and sat on my bed in disbelief, watching the smoke billowing out from the top of the tall, mighty building.

I thought of Bob instantly, who often had meetings at the World Trade Center Towers. Not sure of his schedule on this particular day, I quickly dialed his cell phone. Much to my relief, he answered. He told me that the phones in his office were ringing off their hooks and that several of his co-workers were trying to install a TV to see what was happening at the towers. Bob also reported that he had talked to our son Rob, who was working on repairs on the Manhattan Bridge, and that he was safe.

While on the phone with Bob, I watched in horror as the second plane crashed into the South Tower at 9:03 a.m. I instantly thought New York City was being attacked.

"Bob, we are going to be at war." I continued with my voice quivering, "We must pray for the people in the towers and their families."

I could hear a lot of commotion in the background at Bob's office, so I told him to go and that we would talk when all calmed down around him later.

The mother hen in me desperately wanted to know that my four children were all safe. I wanted to call Rob for myself. He was twenty-one years old and had recently moved into an apartment on the west side of Midtown Manhattan. I wanted to hear his voice and yearned for him to come home. So, I called.

When he answered his cell, I sputtered out, "Thank goodness, Rob, are you safe?"

"Yes, Mom, I am safe!"

Rob's words put me in a better place. He told me that from where he had been working on the bridge, he had clearly seen one of the planes hit the South Tower. The City of New York and the Department of Transportation ordered all bridges to close down, so within fifteen minutes their work was completed. Rob told me businesses of all kinds were closing around him. He added that he had taken the last subway train across town before the subways had shut down, too. He was now hustling toward his Midtown Manhattan apartment, located on the West Side Highway at the end of Forty-second Street and on the river across from the USS *Intrepid*. I told him to stay safe and, if possible, to keep in touch with us, or any of our family members. He said his cell service was sketchy, but he would try to reach me later. I told him that hopefully we would meet for a family dinner the following night if he could get out of the city.

As soon as I hung up my phone, it rang again. My neighbor Karen Livingston told me that her children's school was closing and thought maybe my son Tim's was, too. She asked if we could drive together to pick up her children and then go on to Delbarton School to get Tim. I agreed.

Karen and I were in a sad state of panic riding in the car together, wanting to know more about how this terrifying event could have occurred. We spoke of the families who would be afflicted by this heinous act. As we drove up to Karen's children's school, a long car line of moms waited to pick up their children. When Karen's children entered the car, they immediately started asking questions, and plenty of discussion followed on our way to pick up Tim.

As we arrived at Tim's school, we saw boys streaming out to meet their moms and dads. I spotted Tim, and I instantly emerged from the car to kiss and hug my eighth-grader ever so tightly. Just then the Mother's Guild president approached me and asked if I could stay for a while in case any of the boys who remained might need a grief counselor to talk to. I told her I would stay for two hours, and I sent Tim home with Karen and her children.

The boys who were still at the school stayed huddled in the library, glued to the TV. A mass was being offered by one of the priests at Saint Mary Abbey Church. During my brief time at the school, I learned that several families and relatives of the school community had lost loved ones in the towers. And just when I thought the day could not get any worse, someone told me that at 9:37 a.m., a third plane, *American Airlines Flight 77*, had hit the Pentagon, and at 10:07 a.m., *United Airlines Flight 93* crashed in a field in Shanksville, Pennsylvania. Four planes had crashed, with no survivors accounted for.

Oh, this was a really bad day, a really sad day, I thought. Our country was in deep traumatic grief with unimaginable consequences to follow. "Oh, dear God, help us," I prayed silently.

When I arrived home from Delbarton School, I discovered my daughter Jesse lying on the couch in our living room. She had left Montclair State early, where she was in the master's program, because classes were canceled. I could see that she was in distress. A newlywed of only a few months, Jesse had not yet heard from her husband, Bill, who worked in the district close to the World Trade Center. She tried reaching him on his cell phone, but by this time, the cell towers were down. She was very anxious, and rightly so. A few hours later, she received word Bill made contact with one of his relatives and reported that he was on the ferry and planning to take the train home to Metuchen, New Jersey. Bill asked his relative to get in touch with Jesse so she could meet him at the station. When the relative relayed Bill's message to Jesse, I told her that I would drive her to the station in Metuchen. She still seemed shaky; I did not want her on the roads. Luckily, while on the ferry, Bill met a friend who offered to drive him home so we would not have to go to the station.

As I was driving Jesse down Route 287 to her home, the eerie sight of where the World Trade Center once stood came into view in the distance. Even at 4:30 p.m., clouds of smoke still billowed from the horrific disaster. Tears instantly sprang to my eyes at such a sorrowful sight.

My thoughts then turned to our daughter, Kerry, who worked nights at Overlook Hospital in Summit, New Jersey. I had not called her, knowing that she was likely asleep after her shift the night before. She would be waking up to a nightmare. When she eventually woke up, she called us, and we commiserated on the phone. I asked her to join us for a family dinner the following evening when she would be off from work.

My son Rob reconnected with us later in the day. He described the view from his window overlooking the West Side Highway, where people, some covered with ash, walked north away from the disaster. We learned later that Jesse's husband Bill had to be hosed down before entering the ferry.

That night, Bob and I prayed hand-in-hand for the families who lost loved ones. We prayed for the many children going to bed without a parent. A most sorrowful night indeed it would be for all Americans, I thought as the sun set. How would anyone sleep after experiencing a day that was like no other in the history of our nation? It had been the deadliest terrorist attack on our homeland ever, and we were in its midst. This was a day that would surely be remembered always, a day that would live in infamy in the minds and hearts of all Americans.

The Day After

"I will never forget you. I have carved your
names in the palms of my hands."
(Isa. 49:15-16)

The following day after 9/11 schools were closed as well as sporting events postponed or canceled. Places of interests, such as landmarks, and the roads leading up to them were closed. A state of emergency was declared in the states surrounding what was now being called Ground Zero. Churches were open for prayer services. Everywhere we looked American flags were visible with people flying flags from their homes and from their car windows. The American flags on flagpoles all flew at half-staff. Heightened security was in place all around the tri-state area, and we the people were numb and in shock. It seemed like we were living life in slow motion.

Of this I was sure: in the homes of the families who lost loved ones, it must have been a feeling like no other. Time was standing still for most of them, and I surmised, too, that they were frozen in shock and numbness. It was my hope that their friends, family, neighbors, co-workers, and churches would reach out to them in sympathy.

The media kept us informed about the developments related to the horrid event and constantly showed the search and recovery effort at Ground Zero. Scenes of search dogs helping in the effort flashed on our TV screens. Newscasts prominently featured stories of first responder heroes, and we also heard about the final cell phone calls from the victims to their loved ones.

Father Mychal Judge, OFM, a Franciscan friar who was the New York Fire Department chaplain, was among the first bodies recovered. Rescuers found him under the wreckage of the North Tower lobby. Father Judge was killed while administering the sacrament over a firefighter at the scene. His body was laid before the altar of Saint Peter Catholic Church and was the first certified fatality of September 11, 2001. Father Judge is known as the "Saint of 9/11."

Twenty-seven hours after the disaster, one of the dogs found a woman under the debris. She was the last living person recovered. Sadly, we started to learn the names of some of the victims who the first responders had found under the wreckage. Surely there would be many more stories in the dreaded days ahead.

Speaking of the days ahead, we would later learn that it took one hundred days to extinguish the fires around Ground Zero. There would be 293 bodies found dead and intact. Only twenty living people were rescued, including those who miraculously found their own way out of the disaster. They would be known as survivors and would probably be affected by post-traumatic stress disorder. We would also learn that 3,051 children under the age of eighteen no longer had a parent, and they would be among the thousands who had lost a loved one. On average, each victim's family would have ten to twelve family members inflicted with a long-term, painful, traumatic complicated grief reaction. There were so many people in traumatic grief.

Early on the day after 9/11, I went to the grocery store to pick up provisions for our family dinner that night. I observed people everywhere talking in small groups or shopper-to-shopper at the checkout counter about the previous day. My neighbors, friends, and relatives were calling me. Mostly everyone was staying close to home glued to the media coverage. Bob went to work, in case his company was needed.

My children arrived for our family dinner that night as we had planned. We sat around the table and prayed hand-in-hand for the victims in New York City, Arlington, and Shanksville, Pennsylvania. We prayed, too, for their families and all the children in those families who would be without parents, aunts, uncles, grandparents, and special friends. We prayed for our nation, our president, and the first responders and their families.

After the prayer, the room filled with chatter as we shared stories about what each of us had learned since the day before. I had listened to a safety expert on TV who gave some helpful information for everyone during uncertain times. This expert suggested we have a plan of action as a family and that we identify a meeting place in case lines of communication would go out. Developing our family plan became part of our discussion.

We also talked about all of the people we knew personally who had perished, their families, and their losses. A lot of these people our kids had grown up with or went to school with, and ones I had grown up with. Our son-in-law, Bill, mentioned his relative, Thomas Moody, an FDNY fireman, was a first responder and a victim. A sick feeling stirred inside all of us at the devastation and magnitude of loss of life. It was so surreal yet also a nightmare in our minds and hearts as we ended our family time together that night.

The night would be another dread-filled one. As I prepared to sleep, I closed my eyes in prayer, but could not block the events of 9/11 from my mind. Several times I awoke in worry for our country and sadness for the families of 9/11. It was not a good night's sleep.

In the aftermath of 9/11, people came from far and wide to help. For many days fire departments from all over the nation arrived to aid in the recovery. The outreach was unprecedented. The search and rescue dogs continued their work for almost ten days.

The cleanup efforts were monumental, led by union workers, construction workers, ironworkers, and so many others. Heavy construction vehicles were deployed to remove the large jagged pieces of steel. My husband's company, Koch/Skanska, was involved in the cleanup effort. (They had repaired the World Trade Center after the explosion there in 1993.)

For a brief time, Rob, our son worked at Ground Zero as well. He invited me to visit the site one day while I was in the city for a doctor's appointment. When I arrived, I was escorted in my protective gear and hardhat into the area where the firemen were digging. Here at the footprint of one of the towers where the rubble and remnants were slowly being cleared away, I observed firemen on their hands and knees, digging reverently with their fingers into the soil. I could also see the steel bridge ramp that Bob's company had built to move people and machinery in and out of the area.

A certain peace came over me as I stood on that holy ground and prayed. The Family Viewing Platform erected early on after 9/11 for those families who wanted to remember the victims was in front and just above me. I was overwhelmingly moved by the experience, knowing I was standing on the very spot where such a sad mass murder had taken place. I prayed for peace for the many hearts broken by this horrific act. I asked God to enfold his loving arms around the victims and send an abundance of comfort to their families. Tears touched my face thinking of them and their families. I wanted to believe that this hallowed ground could be transformed and rebuilt into a memorial for each and every one of the dearly beloved victims. Then an old familiar Latin slogan came into my mind, *Succisa Virescit* (Having been cut down, it grows back stronger) — this was all I could hope for as I grimly left the site that day.

This sacred place was a reminder of the many people who were robbed from us all way too soon. Many of the dead were young and in the prime of life. We would learn later that a total of 2,606 men and women had perished at the World Trade Center. Including those who died in the other 9/11 attacks, a total of 2,996 people lost their lives.

The cleanup effort at the World Trade Center site would take eight months and nineteen days. The grief and healing process for the victims' families would take so much longer, maybe even a lifetime.

Discerning My Calling

"You are the light of the world. A city set on a mountain cannot be hidden. Nor do they light a lamp and then put it under a bushel basket; it is set on a lampstand, where it gives light to all in the house. Just so, your light must shine before others, that they may see your good deeds and glorify your heavenly Father."
(Matt. 5:14-16)

The Pam Koch I had always known was eager to help others. She was a person who believed that, if you had a light, you should not hide it under a basket, but rather shine it in the darkness. However, now Pam Koch had changed and was apprehensive — the result of breast cancer. My confidence was challenged, and the gifts I once had were under the basket.

Witnessing the horror of 9/11 and realizing the magnitude of grief the families were involuntarily thrust into ignited a spark inside of me, a spark that had been dormant since shortly after my cancer diagnosis. I did not want to jump into the stressful work of grief counseling again, but the thought was there. I felt helpless, yet I kept thinking about forming a support group. I questioned if my body was strong enough. Was my mind sharp enough? I did feel sharper in mind and body, being three years post-chemotherapy. Plus, my body was getting stronger each day from the second surgery, which had been a few weeks before

9/11, but I was not at one hundred percent yet. The Spirit was willing, but the body was weak, and I continued to pray for direction.

One morning, about a week after 9/11, I made the decision to call the mayor's office in New York. I identified myself as a grief counselor and asked the woman who answered the phone if she would relay a request to the mayor. She said she would, so I asked if the mayor could preserve some of the ashes at Ground Zero for the families, in case they might want them. We had no bodies, but this could be a way to ritualize the loss. I learned later that the mayor sent invitations to the families of 9/11 and invited them to a ceremony where he presented them with small mahogany boxes holding ashes from the site. When I learned of this, my eyebrows raised up. (I was fortunate to meet Rudy several years later, and I thanked him for taking this action. Many families attended the ceremony.)

Around this same time, someone shared a little story with me. A woman, who was a nun, lived in an apartment close to Ground Zero. The day after 9/11, she was looking out her window and noticed that her windowsill was thick with ash. She collected the ash into a small box and then went outside and buried the box. After hearing this story, I thought how wise this woman was to recognize those ashes as sacred. So many stories came from 9/11, stories to share with others that would lend to the healing process. Still almost eighteen years later they circulate, and for years to come they will spread over the hills, plains, mountainsides, into the valleys, and along the seashores: everywhere life exists.

On Sunday, September 16, 2001, the atmosphere was somber as we walked in to attend the 10:30 a.m. Mass at Saint James Church in Basking Ridge, New Jersey. In front of the altar stood eleven tall candles, each representing a member of our parish who had died at the World Trade Center. What a powerful vision to behold. The celebrant was Monsignor Capik, the pastor, and he delivered a heartfelt message reminding us of the consoling love of Jesus Christ.

"It would be our faith that will carry us through this difficult time," he said. The people present needed to hear his words desperately, as we were all hurting. It is true that when one person of the Body of Christ suffers, the whole body suffers. After Communion, I knelt down and had a little conversation with God.

"God, You're going to have to give me a verbal invitation on this one, because I'm not going to know if I should be home taking care of myself or if I should offer to help these sad grieving families."

Minutes after my prayer, the final blessing was given, and as I was leaving the church, I could see the Monsignor in the vestibule with a gathering of people surrounding him. Then, before I could get out the door, I saw out of the corner of my eye his finger pointing at me through the crowd.

Monsignor Capik called my name for me to come to him, and he asked if I was well enough to run a support group for the 9/11 families. I became the risk taker, once again, trusting in God that His invitation was coming through Monsignor in extraordinary time. I told Monsignor "yes," but only on the condition that the grief facilitators I had trained prior were on board. I quickly left the church.

Once outside, I raised my eyes to the heavens and said, "Lord, you don't waste any time, do you?"

I remember thinking that it is in the awareness of God always working in your life that there will be invitation. His invitation was so poignant, definite, and profound.

After returning home, I made several calls to our trained grief facilitators, and their responses were all affirmative. They were eager to reach out to the families. I contacted Monsignor after I spoke to the facilitators, and I planned to meet with him the next evening.

All doubt lifted off my shoulders, and I knew that the grace of God would lead me just as I had felt His presence in the past when entering hospice patients' homes, the hospital rooms of the sick, and the nursing homes of the elderly, and embracing the bereaved. I had great confidence that the Spirit would guide me to walk alongside the families of 9/11.

Within a matter of hours, The Saint James 9/11 Bereavement Support Group had been conceived.

Understanding the magnitude of loss our group would be dealing with and also knowing that my physical body was still mending a bit from my recent surgery, I asked my close friend Elise Krevis to help me lead the group. Elise was a young mom and cancer survivor and also closely acquainted with grief. Her seven-year-old son, Reid, had died of a brain aneurysm several years before 9/11. Elise and her husband Dan had come to one of my support groups at Saint Patrick Church through the referral of my previous pastor, Monsignor Amandolare. Over time, I had trained both Elise and Dan to be grief facilitators.

Elise Krevis is just one of those people who truly reflects a model of a Christian, and she is a deeply caring and compassionate person whom I greatly admire and respect. She became my confidanté and fine example of a bereavement minister in her own right. Our friendship grew over time to the point that we even thought alike. Sometimes I thought it, and she had it done before I could mention the idea! Elise would accompany me to the meeting that Monday night.

With Elise by my side and with Monsignor as the captain at the helm of our USS *WTC 9/11 Survivor Ship*, along with God in collaboration with us, all things were possible, I thought.

Monday evening came, and Monsignor Capik looked tired. He should have, after ministering to many families for the last week. He had gone from house to house, day after day, visiting with families. He was a grey-haired man in his late sixties, full of energy and wit. He was totally committed to his priesthood and in love with his God. A compassionate man, he was beloved by the community of Saint James Church. He was well respected in the town of Basking Ridge among his colleagues and by his fellow priests in the Diocese of Metuchen and surrounding area churches. I was blessed the day I met him. He supported me so profoundly during the aftermath of 9/11. He told me whatever I needed to run the group he would be there to help, and that he was.

Monsignor Capik suggested that we have some type of personal contact with the victims' families in our parish as well as a few in our neighborhood and invite them to come to the bereavement support group. We ruled out putting the group meeting in the bulletin or in the altar announcements in order to ensure confidentiality. Plus, by this point, the media had been all over the victims' families. (They even wanted to film at the hospital where one of the mothers would be giving birth.) We decided to send out a letter and sign it from Monsignor Capik and the Bereavement Ministry team. I offered to compose the letter that evening and to hand the draft to the secretary, Susan Lynch, the following day. She would make the copies and prepare the eighteen letters for mailing to our parishioners and several other families from town who had lost loved ones in the tragic event.

I told Monsignor Capik that I wanted to put our group into action by empowering the people. Everyone was feeling helpless, and I wanted to give the people every opportunity to share their gifts. Healing was needed all around us, not only for the families, but also for everyone in the town. The people in the tri-state area were most deeply affected, but our nation also needed healing. So many were consumed in grief, and a lasting imprint had been seared into our nation's heart and memory. Outreach to these families would help the people who aided them to heal themselves and find the solace they needed.

We concluded our meeting with the decision that we would hold our first official meeting on Thursday, October 4, 2001, at 10:30 a.m. The idea was to wait until after all the memorial services ended and the families visiting from out of town returned home. This also gave us enough time to lay the groundwork for the group and to schedule preliminary meetings with the facilitator team and the volunteer team. The Saint James 9/11 Bereavement Support Group was at its threshold.

The day after our meeting with Monsignor, Elise and I paid a visit to Susan Schlichting Lynch, the parish secretary, as planned. This petite, attractive, middle-aged woman with a cute brown pixie haircut was welcoming and pleasant. She was the type of person who had her fingers on the pulse of the parish. I am so grateful to her to this day for her expertise and compassion, as well as her knowledge. In many ways, Susan was a minister to the bereaved herself. She did whatever she could to help us; she was simply invaluable. She aided us along the way, compiling names, taking messages, and setting up room schedules. One day she presented me with a key to a spacious storage closet that was happily accepted — what a gal! She was absolutely marvelous to work with. I have always believed that the secretaries in the churches I worked in were the "hearts of the home." A flashback came into my mind of Vita Lepore and Mary (Chickie) Tracy at Saint Patrick Church in Chatham, New Jersey, who, like Susan, did everything with a joyful heart to spread the ministry to the bereaved.

We handed Susan the invitation letter to print up and mail out to the families. In return, she handed us a list of volunteers who had been calling or leaving messages at the church wanting to help. (On my unlisted phone number at home, I had been receiving calls as well from neighbors and others I knew in the community.) Elise and I divided up the list and returned home to make our phone calls. We planned to thank the volunteers for their outreach and to invite them to a "Special Needs" meeting the following week. We were right on track, taking each moment as it came.

Laying the Foundation

"Behold I am laying a stone…a corner stone, chosen and precious…"
(1 Pet. 2:6)

OUR FACILITIES

One of my desires for the group was to have a comfortable, warm, living-room-type atmosphere in order to put our mission and vision into action. My wishes came true with the newly built Parish Center at Saint James Church; the facility was a dream! Honestly, I even thought to myself that it seemed as if this building was built for our group…as if it were waiting for us.

The newly constructed ground floor entrance from the ample parking lot beyond the edifice made it easy to enter the building. The entrance was important for mothers bringing baby strollers. The large gathering hall was a great place, I thought, for welcoming and registration tables. Three sets of double glass doors led into a spacious meeting room, where the sun streamed in through three rectangular windows on one wall. The room had an inviting and cordial aura with new wall-to-wall, soft green carpeting accented by the khaki earth tone walls and comfortable new couches and chairs. The room even had space to set up more chairs if necessary. The perimeter had room for tables to hold a library, handouts, and refreshments.

Down the hall were several smaller meeting rooms. The room toward the back of the building had many large windows that illuminated the area with natural light and was the perfect spot for the young children's group. Oh, what a gift this vast space was! I had plans to utilize it all and that we did!

"Thank you, God" was all I could think!

THE FACILITATORS TEAM MEETING
SEPTEMBER 20, 2001
THURSDAY: 7:00 p.m.

Before the Bereavement Group meetings took place, we scheduled a "Grief Facilitator Team," meeting. At this meeting, we discussed our mission and vision of how we could help the 9/11 families and address their practical "Special Needs" in a group setting. Childcare was at the top of the list followed by food, paper goods, along with registration forms. Tissue boxes and bottled water were also listed. We decided to offer sign-up sheets for these committees to oversee the needs.

Next, we discussed our plan of action and reviewed their role as facilitators. I told them I planned to introduce them at the first meeting, and they would tell the group what brought them here. I mentioned that they could read the guidelines for the group, and I explained that we would likely break down into small groups. I re-echoed their previous training and stated that their job as a facilitator was to validate, validate, validate, and affirm the feelings of the people wounded in grief. They were trained in active listening skills, never judging, accepting each griever, and meeting them where he or she was "at." Those grieving were individually and uniquely who they were; not all who are grieving are the same, I expressed to them, and those grieving needed to embrace their own feelings. A facilitator also had to be trustworthy and consistently present at the griever's side. Using a non-judgmental approach and ensuring confidentiality, we would enable the group members to open up and feel safe to express their feelings. The trained facilitators would address these families with compassionate, kind hearts of this I was confident, knowing them. They were the "A TEAM" for sure!

THE VOLUNTEERS TEAM MEETING
SEPTEMBER 25, 2001
TUESDAY: 10:00 a.m.

The vision I had in mind for this day was to meet the volunteers and empower and enable them. Many volunteers lived in town, while others came from surrounding communities. John Denver's song, "The Gift You Are," could be heard in our room as the volunteers came through the doors.

While the day was bright and sunny outside, our room was filled with sadness. The volunteers were deeply stricken with grief since many had lost friends and neighbors just two weeks earlier. I swiftly recognized this was a support group in itself, and we decided to meet twice a month early on.

I asked these beautiful people to introduce themselves. We all know that angels are celestial beings, but I was quite amazed at what followed as we went around the room, filled with approximately forty people.

One girl said her name was Angel, and I told her that I was not surprised. As we moved along, another girl said her name was Angel, too.

"No surprise, again," I said, "because I think all your names should be Angel."

"Wait till you see!" responded another voice.

We continued on, and a girl piped up, "My name is Angel."

Then another person called out, "But wait till you hear her last name."

"My last name is "Hand," replied the third Angel.

"What else would it be?" I said.

I then proclaimed the Volunteers Group be called, "The Angel Hands Group!"

After becoming acquainted with each other and realizing we were surrounded by angels we prayed, and I introduced scripture and music. I tried to help them recognize that they would be instruments of God's healing hands by the good works they were about to give freely to these 9/11 families. In turn, I explained, their actions would lend healing to themselves. We explored what we were all feeling and what they could do to help themselves.

Then, I explained that our volunteer group would be broken down into committees to help keep things organized. We displayed over a dozen large yellow legal pads, each boldly marked with the name of a committee: Welcoming, Hospitality, Hospitality Volunteer Coordinators, Infants and Small Childcare, Volunteer Coordinator for the Infant and Childcare, Secretary, Librarian, Older Children's Group, Hospitality for Children's Group, Pampering, and Floral. We asked those present to sign up for a committee by writing their names and contact information on the paper. The pages were eagerly filled.

Now that our team of facilitators and our team of volunteers had met, the foundation was laid for The Saint James 9/11 Bereavement Support Group to begin. The next week would consist of preparations and solidifying the group's vision, mission, and goals before the first meeting with the families. We were moving consistently forward in a positive way.

The Mission and Vision

HEALING YOURSELF COMES IN TWO STAGES –
First releasing the energy of the suffering, then replacing it with
the soul's energy. It is a gentle and fragile path, very much like
holding on to a thread as it leads you from step to step.
DEEPAK CHOPRA

The Order of Christian Funerals: "If one member suffers in the body of Christ, which is the church, all members suffer with that member." When a member of Christ's Body dies, the faithful are called to a ministry of consolation to those who have suffered the loss of one whom they love. Thus, Christian consolation is rooted in that hope that comes from faith in the saving death and resurrection of Jesus Christ. My team recognized our duty as Christians taken from the *Order of Christian Funerals*. With this in mind, we would embark on our mission to help others.

Our mission plan was to point the way to hope, healing, and transformation. All hopefulness comes through the actions that make it happen, and, with sympathy as well as empathy in our hearts, hope would come. With each support group meeting, we would be keeping this hope alive. We would give these 9/11 families a safe place to release their energy of suffering.

One of my favorite quotes from the Bible is as follows:

"Open your petals, like roses planted near running waters. Send out the fragrance like incense, and put forth blossoms like a lily. Scatter the fragrance, and sing a hymn of praise; bless the Lord for all His works! (Sir. 39:13-14)

I have gone many places on my journey to scatter the fragrance of Christ's Bereavement Ministry — preschools, elementary schools, high schools, special education schools, a local college — and I trained and addressed deacons, seminarians, a deanery of the Catholic Church, hospital hospice volunteers, and doctors, as well as the Girl Scouts of America, senior citizens, nursing homes, and churches of several denominations, to name a few. I knew I had made the right decision to be a volunteer after 9/11. My strong faith, as well as a deep spirit of patriotism, drew me in this direction. How valuable and fragile were the lives we were entrusted with. We as a team felt honored to stand alongside the families of 9/11, our sisters and brothers, and fellow Americans. Our desire was to aid their wounded spirits, souls and trembling hearts and to help lift them up from the darkness into the light and healing in Christ's name. This was our mission.

This world has such a need for grief counseling. Those who choose it as a profession are never without work. This field is a life experience that will enrich the counselor's own life, making it deeper, fuller, and more meaningful in many ways. Always being aware of burnout is important for every caregiver.

VISION/SUPPORT GROUP MODEL/GOAL

The support group model I planned to use was one I had devised early on in my work with bereavement groups and continued to develop over the years. The title of the model was, "Journey from Grief into Hope." My vision included a faith-based, educational support group that focused on the body, mind, and spirit. My desire was to address the grievers with this holistic approach, which had worked well over the years whenever I implemented it.

Christ's compassion had to be at our team's very core and our foundation. The sincere spirit of compassion in the hearts of the volunteer and grief facilitator team members would then overflow into a catalyst for hope, healing, and transformation. These bereaved families would not grieve as those who had no hope. The path for the 9/11 families would be baby steps and wobbly in the beginning, but stronger with two secure feet on the ground, hopefully, toward the end of our time together.

Through education and support, we believed that the grievers' compasses would be pointed toward our end goal in mind — a transformative grief reaction.

I planned to measure the success of our group by the commitment the members showed through their attendance. In time, I would ask attendees to fill out an evaluation form. Additionally, I would spot check members, calling them in the off time, because listening all the time was crucial. The real success story would be evident when the group was over. I have watched deeply broken spirits make the choice to work on their grief while leaning into the pain and telling their story of loss in a safe place, helping to soften the edges of their grief. When the resilient self emerges and seeks to make great strides in the world birthing their loved one's name back into the world in another way, not only for themselves, but also for others, the results are always positive. This is what I call transformation or transformative grief in action. I have witnessed amazing accomplishments while working on transformative grief or perhaps what Deepak Chopra might call the soul's energy. I sometimes think of them as miracles.

My mind continued to spin during the days leading up to our first group meeting. I knew this group would continue for longer than any group I had ever run. This was because of the mode of death being public grief and mass murder, a sudden traumatic death, and all the intricate feelings that resulted for those who lost loved ones. In the assumptive world of the griever, prior hopes and dreams were no longer. I would have time to teach them more about the traumatic complicated grief process they were dealing with. They in turn would be my teachers as my dying patients were in my hospice work; an education far beyond any textbook could accomplish. They would have the time to explore and discuss all those feelings affecting them. I knew the reality of the lost was just not there. I knew we were giving the families a safe place to release their emotional pain, and we would give them, also tools to help them live each day. This would be another step. Exploring thoughts and belief's would play a big part. I started working on a plan of action. I wanted the families to know everything about the grief process they were experiencing. I wanted, them, to express their feelings with each concept and help them work through their grief.

During the first few meetings, I planned to address and explore the spiritual self. In this modern world filled with many distractions, some people may not take the time to nurture their spiritual inner self. I already knew that my group would consist of people from different denominations, mainly Christian plus several Jewish members. I thought about how many people, at a time of tragedy, need someone to blame, and God always seems to be the one. People ask, "Why, God, why? How could you ever allow this to happen?" I had uttered those words almost two decades earlier when my sister Joan died, and I had been hearing those words over and over in the weeks since 9/11. The evil that reared its ugly head on 9/11 came through the acts of terrorists, not God. Those terrorists had free will, and their choices were filled with a deep-rooted, twisted, hateful ideology. My hope was that our team and the "people of goodness" who would surround the families of 9/11 would draw them into an even closer and deeper relationship with their loving God, their "Yahweh."

I wanted the group members to explore, "Who is God for you?" Then I would discuss the foundation of our Judeo-Christian faith belief system that God is the center of all goodness and love. God had created everyone in the group, and the same God also created their loved ones who had died. They were all God's own artwork,

God's children, and God was filled with immeasurable, infinite, and unconditional love for each and every one of them. "Abba," had not and would not abandon them. Our loving Father was living in their broken hearts and cried the many tears with them. I recalled a homily once given by my friend, Father Peter Krebs the question God might be asking us is "Where are you?" God may answer, "Come home to me to the center of your heart where love and God reside." My job, so to speak, was to guide them into turning on their heart lights. I often told them I was just there to turn on the lights. They were doing all the work! "Turning on the lights" had a deeper meaning for me.

Once we had established and reviewed the spiritual aspect of grief, we would build on that so the families would recognize that this grief not only affected their spiritual self, but also their physical, emotional, cognitive, and behavioral self. I wanted these families to be careful driving. I wanted them to pamper themselves. I wanted them to eat well and drink plenty of water. I wanted them to have a one-on-one therapist. (I would share with them that I was a certified pastoral bereavement counselor, not a licensed therapist) I wanted them to keep journals and planned to assign them buddies within the group. I wanted them to have tools to address their body, mind, and spirit.

I wanted them to know that if they thought they were going crazy, it was a common feeling and something I had heard over and over again in my years as a counselor. Grief can send a person into utter chaos, and it is natural to think that you are going crazy from time to time. I planned to explain that the experience of a traumatic complicated loss results in bereavement overload. Of course, I wanted to explore with them the **Positive** verses **Negative Coping Mechanisms** since these were a must! I wanted them to know that they had choices, and just their being in the room was a positive one. I wanted them to be aware of the terms associated with grief, such as **Anticipatory Grief, Residual Grief, Unresolved Grief, Delayed Grief, Disenfranchised Grief,** and **Transformative Grief**. I planned to explore the differences between **Normal Grief** verses **Complicated Grief**.

Another one of my desires was for the families to know my teachers and the theorists in the field of bereavement. The term Thanatology, derived from the Greek word *Thanatos*, refers to the science that examines the attitudes and the meaning and behaviors of bereavement and grief. I hoped to share with them the theory of Dr. Elizabeth Kubler-Ross and her *Five Stages of Grief* she writes about in her book *On Death and Dying*. Here she names these stages as tools as part of a framework to help those to learn to live with the loss of a loved one. Early on she opened up dialogue in the field of Death and Dying. I wanted them to know about Dr. J. William Worden's, *Four Tasks of Mourning*, talked about in his book, *Grief Counseling and Grief Therapy*. I wanted to explore with them Dr. Kenneth Doka's theory on **Disenfranchised Grief** found in his book *Disenfranchised Grief: Recognizing Hidden Sorrow*. I wanted to touch on the *Six R Processes*, the theory of Dr. Therese Rando. I also thought about *The 7 Habits of Highly Effective People*, written by Stephen R. Covey. This idea stemmed from a course I had taken at the University of Notre Dame in South Bend, Indiana, and I had used this model in prior groups and I would certainly use it in this group. I would adapt it to **7 Habits for Highly Effective People in Grief**.

So much was on my agenda, but I knew we were only at the beginning and needed to take one step at a time. All that I wanted was good, but I needed to be cognizant that the families would steer the way. Each group that I had worked with over thirteen years had built their own identity. The days ahead would reveal this to be true of the 9/11 families, too. In the beginning, the families would be noticeably numb and in shock, so we would step softly and gently, weaving the golden threads of life past and the silver threads to their future on the fragile path toward hope, healing, and transformation. Taking each day as it comes was the plan. Slowly, gently, with sympathy, empathy, compassion, and patience, we would walk beside these hurting families to help ameliorate their pain.

Chapter 10

Goodness Defined and Accounted For

GOODNESS: *Easton's Bible Dictionary*
"One of the fruits of the indwelling Spirit of God."
Gal.: 5:22
GOODNESS: *Webster's Dictionary*
"The quality of being good, moral excellence;
virtuousness, kindness."
GOODNESS: *Merriam-Webster Dictionary*
"Something conforming to the moral order of the universe."

The following chapters are an account of the "Goodness" I witnessed from people of The Saint James 9/11 Bereavement Support group, "Journey from Grief into Hope." I was most honored and privileged to work with these 9/11 families, as well as being present to witness the profuse "Goodness" that was bestowed unconditionally on them by volunteers and strangers.

During our time together, I kept a journal, and the more I wrote, the more I realized that it was "Goodness" I was writing about and that the outpouring of love needed to be documented. The people who surrounded these families are the ones I consider to be the "People of Goodness." The center of all "Goodness" was present; it was God surely being manifested, shining radiantly through these people in the grandest of ways during the darkest of days.

The following begins the account of our support group meetings. Woven throughout my account are the reflections of our volunteers. I share with you, with permission, the impact this experience had on several of their lives.

OCTOBER 4, 2001
THURSDAY: 9 a.m.
BEHIND THE SCENES

A couple of weeks before the meeting, I had asked the art teacher, Diane Lopez, at Delbarton School in Morristown, New Jersey, where my son Tim attended, to make a welcome poster to place next to the registration desk. This large green poster, the color for hope, beautifully adorned with a rainbow and the name of our group, "Journey from Grief into Hope," greeted the families as they entered the foyer. I also asked, the art teacher at the Oak Knoll School in Summit, New Jersey, Will Cardell, to create a poster of all the victims' names from our area. On a large board, he created a masterpiece of red, white, and blue, with gold stars after each name listed on it. (We would add more names to the board as more and more people joined the group.) The board was placed in the front of the meeting room with flowers and candles before it. This simple setup created a place for ritual that was especially helpful and aided in the grieving process.

While planning for the first meeting, I added the word "candles" to the top of my shopping list since I needed to purchase some for ritual. After adding candles to my list, I started returning the weekly phone messages given to me by Susan, the church secretary. I dialed the first number on the list even though it appeared to be an out-of-state number. A young woman answered the phone, and I introduced myself. She told me that she owned a candle-making company in Maine and wanted to contribute a gift of candles to us, in the hope that she could help the families in some way. How timely, but not a coincidence, I thought, that this thoughtful stranger from Maine would be lighting our path! Our group was not publicized — she must have found out about our group through word of mouth. No coincidence!

Now, on the morning of our meeting, those candles burned at the front of the room, and the aroma of coffee wafted in the air. The stage was set for Day One! The groundwork had been accomplished. All of our elves had been busy at work! The volunteers had come through big time. Goodness was spinning in action all around.

The facilitators and the Welcome Committee stood waiting at the doors with open arms. Our volunteer leaders for the Hospitality Committee, Chris Green and Angel Hand, had their food committee in full energy, lots of home-baked goodies, including, a scrumptious homemade banana bread (made by Karen Newhouse, a weekly baker and volunteer), adorned decorated tables, and a bountiful lunch, provided by The Madison Hotel in Madison, New Jersey, awaited us.

Betsy Schulenburg, a young mom and member of our church at Saint James, had created and organized an outstanding library of books on loss and bereavement. Authors from all over the nation sent us copies of their books. Compassion Books, a resource I had used often in the past, sent us many issues of their publications. Several area bookstores gave us donations, including an especially generous one from The Bookworm in Bernardsville, New Jersey.

I suggested to Betsy that one way to enable people, who felt helpless and wanted to do something for the families, would be to suggest donations of books about grief. Many people made donations in the victims' names, and those names, along with the name of the family who donated each book, were inscribed on the attractive labels that Betsy had created for inside the front covers. In addition to creating the book labels, Betsy made captivating signs for the adult section, as well as for the children's section. Her library was abundantly overflowing, and so she extended it with more tables. Betsy, who took her volunteer position to heart, even planned to attend workshops to enhance her work.

Next to Betsy's library tables, several other tables, dressed in yellow and green tablecloths, were piled high with booklets and brochures on trauma and for children in trauma. This was an outpouring of goodness with the "wow" factor at hand! My neighbor, Kris Klingert, and also Carol Mottes, signed up to help on her team.

Pat McNamee, a friend of mine, and Carol Mottes, a neighbor of one of the 9/11 families, both wanted to reach out to the families and volunteered to serve in the registration area. They warmly greeted the families in the gathering foyer and registered them as they came through the doors. I had become friends with Pat and her family a couple of years earlier while doing hospice care with her sweet mother, Eileen, who was terminally ill with cancer at the time. Pat and her sister, Eileen, attended my bereavement support group at Saint Patrick Church after their mother's death. She was a member of Christ The King Church in nearby New Vernon, New Jersey, where several more of the families who had lost loved ones in 9/11 were members. Later, when one of my facilitators needed to leave for a personal issue, Pat was trained as a facilitator.

Fran O'Brien, a widow from our church, came to help too. She had been a member of the original Bereavement Team at Saint James. Fran wanted to give aid to these young families and knew how difficult it was to lose a spouse. She changed her job schedule at the Shrine of Saint Joseph to work with us. She was invaluable as a trained facilitator.

Another member of our team, Mary Hess, was a trained chaplain from Memorial Sloan Kettering Cancer Center in New York City. Later, Mary was very active in working to aid a local breast cancer organization in Summit, New Jersey. We were lucky to have her with us. She was a great gift.

Staci Sykoff was a neighbor of mine and the mother of two little girls. She was a social worker who wanted to reach out to the families in some way. We welcomed her with open arms.

Alexis Carola, who ran mothers' retreats in the parish, was eager to help as well. She had trained as part of our original Bereavement Team at Saint James. Alexis, was a loving individual who was simply a pleasure to have as part of our facilitator team.

Our Infant and Childcare Coordinator, Liz Bagnoto, was a young mom filled with lots of energy. She had the young children's group set up down the hall in a brightly lit room organized with several volunteers, as well as with toys, juice packs, and childlike snacks. Julie Lee, Margaret Cahill, Pat Gilbreth, Ginger Menichillo, Carol Galgano, Michelle Quinn, Eileen Magno, Barbara Madaio, Jeanne Finn, Brigid Dolan, Betty Moore, and Kathleen K., were the "All-Star Team" of volunteers among the many. These women enveloped the young children in their loving arms, many of them moms themselves. With big hearts made of gold and a nurturing spirit, they did what they do best — caring for the young children.

Lori Velasco oversaw the Pampering Committee, an extremely creative and much-appreciated group. They organized the special services — spa days, massage appointments, salon donations, and the like — donated from area stores to help pamper the group. Carol Mottes and Carol Galgano were our Volunteer Coordinators. What would we have done without these girls? "Fantastic" is the word to describe them.

Our secretary, and publicity chairwoman, Prudence Pigott, sent out a multitude of letters of gratitude to a myriad of people who reached out to us. Prudence was one of the parishioners of Saint James Church and a Delbarton School tennis mom who had a son in my son's class at the school. She could run any business just superbly! I was so lucky to have her as part of the team. Prudence was a capable person in an abundance of ways. She would be outstanding for any job.

Flowers brightened the room on the day of our first meeting, thanks to our Floral Committee. With the goodness from area florists and nurseries, we were mesmerized by the color, fragrance, and beauty not only on the first day, but also for the two years that our group would be together. Volunteers, Mary and Michael Ryan, trimmed our room with comfort, helping to tamp the gloom.

Lots of water bottles and tissue boxes were dotted around the room and were generously donated to us by a friend who owned a food franchise in Linden, New Jersey. George Abad's generosity supplied us abundantly. This man was awesome!

Jane Mitchell and Sue Ably were two incredible nurses from the parish team who were available to me when I needed them. Their expertise as parish nurses was immeasurable during that time.

To say I had good support all around me would be an understatement. Every one of the volunteers helped make our group what it was. All of the volunteers were dynamic and priceless. They were steadfast by our side, ready to produce whatever was needed and often juggling multiple tasks. The group could never have run so smoothly without them. Even the bathrooms were decorated with flowers, special hand towels, and candles. This was an amazing group of admirable top-notch human beings.

My apologies to anyone and everyone I have overlooked here as committee chairs and aides. There were just so many of you at every turn. Please know there were many more volunteers too numerous to mention, but always in our hearts. Thank you everyone.

The goodness was darting all around, like sparks of light steadily upon us. I believe it was truly the "Spirit of Goodness." The Spirit of God was never far away from us and was oh, so close on that dismal first day when we met the families of 9/11.

REFLECTIONS FROM ELISE KREVIS, CO-COORDINATOR

I joined The Saint James Bereavement Support Group as a trained group facilitator at the time of 9/11. It is hard to express the impact that this role had on my life. For me, the call of compassion is when people come to the aid of others in their time of tragedy and personal pain. It is a witness to God's real presence in our world.

On September 30, 1998, I lost my son Reid suddenly at the age of seven. It was an unthinkable loss with the shock and grief overwhelming every facet of my life. Family, friends, acquaintances, and even strangers answered the call of compassion to carry me through the long journey of grief to healing. I knew then that I was touched by others' goodness and the call for me to give back had become clear.

Along my journey, I met Pam Koch at a bereavement support group I joined in Chatham, New Jersey, and shortly thereafter, Pam moved to Basking Ridge. There she offered to help train a team to form a bereavement support group for our parish, and she met with Monsignor Capik to discuss the program. Monsignor reconnected Pam with me, and I answered the call of compassion to support this new group as a facilitator. So powerful were the overlapping coincidences of people and events in my life that would guide me to reach out to others.

When the 9/11 tragedies occurred, we were in place over a year and quickly transitioned to The Saint James 9/11 Bereavement Support Group. There I witnessed those wounded in grief, men and women, reaching out and holding each other up, providing comfort and support. We worked as a group to bring about healing and never could I believe how far we went.

If the group only knew at the time of their grief how they touched my life and strengthened me in my Christian belief and in my own healing from the tragic loss of my small son Reid several years earlier. How moved and blessed my family was when one of the 9/11 women gave birth to a baby boy and named it after our son Reid.

I continue to honor and give memory to my Reid's life and love, his beautiful smile and joy of living, by reaching out to others on their journey of grief. I am hoping that they too will feel these same things from the lives of those they lost and the compassion of the people who will reach out to them. With faith, compassion, and love, I pray for all of us each and every day.

God Bless.

"Journey from Grief into Hope" is born

Hope is that thing with feathers
That perches in the soul,
And sings the tune without the words,
And never stops at all.
Emily Dickinson

THE MEETINGS BEGIN
October 4, 2001
THURSDAY: 10:30 a.m.
19 - men and women in attendance

After attending mass, I walked into our meeting room filled with confidence, courage, hope, and strength. These families would have hope, and our team was going to be instruments of God who would guide them on their "Journey from Grief into Hope."

As I looked around the room, I counted nineteen people mingling, some with coffee cups in hand. The mood was somber and filled with hugs and quiet conversation. To me, the group seemed bonded before we even sat down. Several of the women wore large buttons over their hearts bearing images of their loved ones. Many were dressed in jeans and t-shirts. There were a few older men and women present, maybe parents and family members of the younger women present, I thought. (Later, I would learn that they had lost their sons.)

Monsignor Capik asked the families to come together to begin the meeting. After offering some consoling words, he introduced his associate priest, Father Jay, and talked about the plan for the support group. Monsignor Capik then introduced me, and I welcomed the group and expressed our deepest sympathies on behalf of our team. I told the group who I was, that I was new to the parish, and that I was a wife and a mother of four. I told of how I had experienced many losses in my own life and how I was trained in hospice and had been on the staff of Saint Patrick Church in Chatham for the last thirteen years during which time I trained and worked as a certified pastoral bereavement counselor. I talked about my experience coordinating support groups for the bereaved and working with adults, children, and teens. However, I emphasized that I was not a licensed therapist, but I did have referral cards available for local area therapists.

I then transitioned into a scripture —

"Suddenly a violent storm came up on the sea, so that the boat was being swamped by waves; but he was asleep and they came and woke him saying "Lord, save us! We are perishing!" Then He said, "Why are you so terrified, O you of little faith?" Then he got up, rebuked the winds and sea, and there was great calm."
(Matt. 8:24–26)

After reading the gospel and some consoling words, I transitioned once again into soft, soothing music. Faint sniffles could be heard around the room. After a moment of silence, I asked the facilitators to come to the front of the room so everyone could see their faces. The team introduced themselves and briefly told their stories talking about what had brought them to the Bereavement Team.

Since I knew the grief work was going to be time-consuming, we took care of group business first. Elise read the group guidelines, and we looked at what day and time would be best for everyone to meet. We voted on Thursdays at 10:30 a.m.

After that, I talked about the three "C's" — **Commitment, Confidentiality,** and **Crying.** I asked the families to make a **Commitment** to themselves for the first three meetings, and if our program did not work for them, that would be okay. I encouraged them to seek help elsewhere if they decided to not return to our group. I stressed that **Confidentiality** was crucial in the group. I explained that **Crying** is part of the pain, opening up and cleaning out the wounded spirit within. I affirmed their humanness and told them it was okay to cry at any time. I added that there could be moments when we might even laugh in the group, for laughter, too, can be used appropriately.

Next, I invited the families to introduce themselves and say why they were there. I gave them permission to pass if they needed to do so. We listened to their heart-rending stories and the outpouring of excruciating acute grief. We learned that our group consisted of spouses of those who had perished, parents who had lost children, fiancés who had lost those they were engaged to marry, and two sisters who had both lost their spouses, and several siblings including one who had lost a brother who was a passenger on the *United Airlines flight 175* out of Boston. We gave those who chose to speak all the time that they needed. Listening with a compassionate heart was what we were there for. As individuals spoke, I made notes of special needs.

After a short break, I continued with An **Overview of Grief.** I began by explaining that loss is part of the human condition. It is the change in familiar patterns in our lives. Grief is the reaction to loss, those feelings of knots inside us that seem to linger on. Grief can result from a loss of any kind. You may lose your keys, your eyeglasses, your cell phone, your wallet, or maybe even your Apple ID. Grief on a deeper level can result from the loss of a job, a beloved pet, maybe the loss of a relationship, or a divorce of a marriage. Then there is the death of a loved one, which leads the griever into a process of mourning, and into an even longer process of grief called bereavement. I believe bereavement results from all of the above not just death of a loved one. Secondary losses can result after a loss, e.g., the loss of hopes and dreams, the loss of the person who paid the bills, or the loss of financial stability to stay in the family home. These secondary losses just seem to tag along with the loss unfortunately, for many people.

Mourning is a period of time for rituals, such as wakes, funeral rituals, and memorials. We sometimes say that mourning is grief gone public. People who are grieving may wear black during this time. In some countries, such as in England traditions of mourning are practiced with the bereaved wearing "mourning armbands." In Ireland, "mourning wreaths" trimmed in black bows might be placed on the front doors of people's homes where a death has occurred. Grievers in Italy can be seen wearing black for an extended period of time. In the United States and elsewhere, flags were flown at half-staff after 9/11. All of these actions are expressions of mourning.

The bereavement process takes considerably longer time than mourning. I explained to the group that bereavement was a complex and intricate process. You enter the bereavement process with your suitcase of who you are, unique unto yourself — your family background, your faith belief (if any), your stage in life, your age, and your gender. No two people grieve alike. When I counsel, I often ask grievers how their parents might have taught them to grieve or maybe they tried to protect their child from the pain of loss. There is no right way to grieve nor is there a wrong way to grieve. There is only your way to grieve.

Grief has no time limit. People say, "time will heal," but I am a firm believer that it is what a person does with that time that will help to accelerate the healing process. Grief affects a person spiritually, physically, emotionally, mentally, and socially. The grief process is hard work, and it is draining. It is very hard work, perhaps the hardest work a person will ever have to do. Some people get stuck or decide not to take on this taxing work, hoping that grief can be swept under the rug. This approach is often problematic as life unfolds. The grief always resurfaces. The healthiest option is to deal with the grief up front, to unravel those knots, to resolve the grief, and to talk about it with others, such as those in our group. Leaning into the pain is a good way to deal with grief; you cannot go around it, you cannot go over or under grief — you can only go through it.

I then explained to the 9/11 families that they were experiencing what is called a traumatic complicated grief. This kind of grief takes longer than a normal grief and is known as bereavement overload. I said that we would explore the concept more in detail in the coming days.

I told the story I often tell about a woman I met in a support group who told me that she had had seven new jobs in the seven years since her husband died. She realized listening to my talk that she had never really grieved. I believed she was experiencing a delayed grief. I put her right to work! Grief will always resurface whether in relationships with others, or in the workplace, as it was in her case.

The grief's physical manifestations are first to appear at the time of loss. They come in many forms — feelings of shock and numbness, lack of appetite, nausea, vomiting, sweating, feeling faint or shaky, sleep disturbances, PTSD, (post-traumatic stress disorder) headaches, loss of voice, panic attacks, etc. Several of these manifestations can also be the first to leave after the shock and numbness wear off. I suggested to them to ask friends to drive them places they needed to go or do errands for them, maybe pick up or deliver the children for just a couple of weeks. One of our members had already been in an accident.

It is important to take breaks from grief, and I really recommend it. I explained further, "You can do this by being kind to yourself, pampering yourself, or treating yourself to a massage. You can take walks or exercise and listen to soft music, all of which may help you sleep better. Maybe go to a movie or buy a new outfit, and be sure to eat well and drink plenty of water. For those of you with children, allow them to have breaks from grief, too, by going to the movies or planning a playdate." Children are thought of as the silent grievers. They don't grieve the way adults do. They look to be doing O.K. at times. Every, child's grief needs to be address on their developmental level. We will go further into discussion at the up coming meeting on "Children In Grief."

We have choices, healthy choices in grief. One choice everyone in the group made that day was to be here, and that is certainly a positive coping choice. It is in telling the story that we are healed. Having a person to listen to you, without judgment, a person experiencing the same kind of loss as yours, is also helpful. That is why support groups can be beneficial.

I continued on by telling the families to be cognizant that anger can play a large part in a traumatic complicated grief. I assured them we would touch on this in more detail. No yardstick is long enough to measure how deeply each person loved the person who died. I, myself, was angry that such beautiful people as themselves, had to endure this tragedy. I commented once again on the media. Watching the media coverage on TV could pull you in and out of grief. Maybe the better choice is a bubble bath. I asked them to try avoiding the media if possible, and for their children's sake too.

I finished with some final pieces of advice — "Take each day as it comes; be especially kind to yourself right now and let us help you if there is a need. Make an appointment with your doctor to explain what has happened to you."

The day was very hard and emotional for the families. The room was full of broken spirits and overflowing with tears as we swayed, arm-in-arm in a circle, rocking to soothing prayerful music. We ended the day, after almost four hours, with a candle-lighting ceremony of light and love.

While I did not know one person there, I knew that their hearts were visibly broken. I noticed, too, that the group hardly ate even though we had an abundance of food for refreshments and for lunch. It was a long, hard day, a day that only affirmed to myself, and my team that we were on sacred and holy ground.

After the families left, my team and I processed out together. "Processing out" and "Processing in" are terms I use in my work with bereavement group grief counseling. "Processing out" occurs after the meeting when the group leader and individuals sit down in a quiet area and talk about the experience of being in the room. We discuss how the experience affected each of us and what those feelings were like for us. "Processing in" occurs before an individual, who is a guest or presenter, enters the group meeting room for the first time or with the facilitator team. This brief session helps prepare those who have never been in the group setting before for what will be encountered. We discuss the atmosphere they will experience and what to expect. I am aware that stepping into a room with so many people in grief at one time might be overwhelming for an individual, and my desire is to help each person be as comfortable as possible. For the 9/11 meetings, I tried to welcome and meet the presenters myself beforehand to process them in as well as process them out afterward.

On a personal level, I processed out with a therapist after the meetings for several weeks until time restraints in my schedule detoured me. I regularly exercised; went for walks at Harry Dunham Park; went for massages; soaked in lots of bubble baths; listened to soft music and the Benedictine Monk chants; participated in journaling, meditation, and prayer; and took several long weekend trips to Cape Cod and the sunshine state, Florida.

The morning after our first meeting I sat at my desk glancing at the notes on my legal pad. The word in my head was **FOCUS**. There was so much to take in, and I had to focus on the most important areas first. The heading on the pad was **SPECIAL NEEDS** and underlined. The word **CHILDREN** was written boldly and underlined. One other word jumped out — **PAPERWORK.**

In prior groups that I had run, the paperwork was a nemesis, and now it was becoming so in this group. I knew the amount of paperwork was going to be even more magnified for the 9/11 families, given the nature of the deaths and the enormity of the loss. I recalled asking a prior bereavement group at Saint Patrick Church several years earlier to transform their grief and write a handbook on, *Paperwork during the Grief Process*, to help others in the future. I challenged them to give it to me for my birthday. Sure enough, later that year on my birthday, they came into one of my group meetings with a cake, and forty copies of a book they had written entitled, *The Paper Chase*. I was so proud of them, I screamed! I only wished we might have published that informative book! I also wished I had a copy left to share with my 9/11 families. The paperwork would be similar in some aspects but, because of the *Victims Compensation Fund* forms among many others related to the circumstances of the deaths, the paperwork would be more complex than for a normal death occurrence.

I knew the paperwork was beginning to overwhelm the families, and I knew I could find people to help them. A short time later, at an opportune time, I received a phone call from a very nice gentleman named, Carl Quick who offered his assistance to the group. He was a member of the Saint Vincent De Paul Society at Our Lady of Perpetual Help in Bernardsville, New Jersey.

Carl and I set up a date for coffee, and at this meeting, he offered to be an advocate for helping families with their paperwork. He was a great guy and truly a person of integrity. I instantly took him up on his offer and put him right to work.

While thinking about the children issues, I truly questioned if I could do a children's group myself. We had an amazing group of volunteer ladies caring for the babies and toddlers, but the older children would benefit from an organized children's group. Personally, I loved running children's groups. I loved working with children in art therapy, one of the avenues I used to help them express their grief and emotions. I loved their resiliency and their literal innocent insight. After some thought, I decided that it was just not possible. Running a children's group would be way too much of a strain on me physically after my surgery and procedures. The very next day, Monsignor Capik handed me a resume, and I read it over carefully.

Karen M., one of our gifted parishioners, was a trained professional Child Life Specialist with a master's degree in Special Education, and she offered to help run a group for our children. She worked at JFK Hospital as a child trauma specialist where, according to her resumé, she used visual arts and play therapy, among other modalities. I called her and set up a meeting. She said she could make the commitment to the group, and she had great ideas. I invited her to make a presentation at our October 18th meeting to address the parents, introduce her program, and answer questions. The adult group meeting would be labeled "Children In Grief."

In the weeks to come, Karen would create a young children's group and later start a teen group. Patty Lunny who was a volunteer from Saint Mark Episcopal Church in town eagerly signed up to head hospitality for the children's group. She was an enthusiastic volunteer and aide for Karen and the children.

One thing I requested of Karen and the children's group was a children's art show to be held in the spring. The children's artwork would be displayed after the masses at Saint James Church for all of the parishioners to see.

Returning to the morning after our first meeting, I sat at my desk and as I thought about my next steps, I knew the group needed some answers. For one, I planned to dig deeper into my file of speakers who could help move the group forward. The second step would be a bigger challenge. I wanted to take the group to visit Pier 94 in New York City. Pier 94, which I had learned about from a television program, was a place set up as a Family Center to aid the bereaved relatives and surviving workers of the World Trade Center disaster. Every government agency was present there and had booths set up to help. Some local families had already been there, courtesy of Captain Robert Kumpf of the Basking Ridge Police Department, but many of our members did not want to go into the city; they had a real phobia about it. I wanted to see Pier 94 for myself and planned to do so after our next meeting.

REFLECTIONS FROM ALEXIS CAROLA, A FACILITATOR

The role I played with the 9/11 widows, widowers, fiancés, mothers, and fathers was one of a facilitator at our Church of Saint James in Basking Ridge, New Jersey. We had lost many men in our parish, but our group was open to all who lost loved ones on that awful day. Many came from literally all over the state.

I have thought often of that momentous time and, in particular, I recall that very first day when we met in a large couched room with several chairs, all filled.

I had met Pam before when I was going through my own grief with my dad's sudden death. I felt confident in her, but also overwhelmed by the magnitude of the "job." It was clear from the first words of the day: we knew that these families would not grieve as those who had no hope. God had truly prepared Pam to guide us to help these hurting families.

We did, week after week we led them forward — giving every person in attendance a chance to share his/her pain. We listened, and we cried.

Going back to that first day, the air was so heavy with tension. The sadness so real, you could feel it, taste it, and touch it. At the end of the meeting, I remember being so distraught. The heaviness – the incredible sadness – that was in the room filled me to my very core, I knew that I needed to be there and to do my very little part in help healing these people.

For the next two years, we pretty much met every Thursday. The families were led in various exercises, stories, thoughts, and sharing wisdom gleaned from the countless similar sessions through the many years of experience of a grief counselor. I marveled at our coordinator's confidence and willingness to aid these individuals and she, in turn, marveled at our team of facilitators for our dedication and compassionate presence to the families.

My part was really just being there, my presence. I remembered my "cue," trying to be the good listener.

Did this "change my life" to continue to reach out in other ways? Paul and I were already very involved at Saint James, so I wasn't looking to do any more "reach-outs." I would hope this experience has made me, more compassionate, more giving, and a better listener.

As far as the impact this experience made on me: The tragedy of that day became very personal for me. As I learned more of the men's and women's stories, I was drawn into their pain and suffering. 9/11 became for me an immense importance, for it gave me an empathetic and sympathetic insight into women longing for their husbands, missing their last call because they were in the shower, children saying the rosary for their dads, not knowing if they were alive or dead, moms in disbelief over the loss of their sons, moms-to-be not knowing how they would bring up their child alone, a dad left to raise three-year-old twins, and fiancés facing their wedding day alone; the incredible anguish on the faces of all.

Embarking toward Hope

"For a tree there is hope, if it is cut down, it will
sprout again, its tender shoots will not cease."
(Job 14:7)

OCTOBER 11, 2001
THURSDAY: 10:30 a.m.
29- in attendance

T his day marked the one-month anniversary of 9/11 and obviously
another difficult day for our group. We went to where they were
"at" on this day.

Our session opened with prayer, scripture, breathing techniques,
and soft music. The room once again was inviting and filled with
flowers, food, and the aroma of the coffee, as well as soothing music.
On this particular day, the families seemed connected and comfortable,
with twenty-nine in attendance, plus many more infants and toddlers.

Massage therapists from the YMCA had called to offer their
services. Realizing how much this could benefit the families, I agreed.
On the day of the meeting, I processed the therapists into the room,
emphasizing the need for confidentiality and describing what they
would be experiencing. We had two massage therapists present, and
their chairs were full throughout the meeting. (These therapists

attended a few of our early meetings due to their work constraints. They worked diligently while there, and I processed them out after each meeting.)

I had an abundance of information to share, but since our numbers had increased, I found myself reviewing the prior week's program over again.

We had received two very helpful donations since our previous meeting. The first was a big message board that stood at the front of the room on which we displayed helpful information. The second donation, were journals donated by a really neat lady, my darling mother, Rita Bundschuh. I explained to the group that I wanted them to write ideas and information down in their journals. At times I planned to give them homework exercises, such as writing a letter to the loved one who had died or a message to God for a great need. Sharing was of the essence for these families, and the journals were the perfect place to keep the relevant information. They wanted to help each other in any way they could with any tidbit they learned while they were away from each other during the week. Part of our job as facilitators was to share the necessary information, keep the meeting flowing, and all the while listening for their needs.

The topic for this meeting was *The Five Stages of Grief*, a theory known as the Kubler-Ross model created by Elizabeth Kubler-Ross, an American (Swiss born) doctor of psychiatry. She was the first of three theorists, in the field, who I wanted to share with the group. Still today I hear her theory talked about when loss occurs. Bereavement creates many intricate feelings. We began our meeting by exploring each of these five stages: Denial, Bargaining, Anger, Depression, and Acceptance. People may not experience all of these stages.

I explained that these stages were like frogs in a basket jumping up and down and all around and the process is not linear. So many other feelings of helplessness and hopelessness would overwhelm these families as part of this bereavement process. It is a messy process, to say the least, and very hard work indeed.

We shared our thoughts and told stories. After four and a half hours, we ended the meeting with another moving candle-lighting ritual and soft music. My agenda was not totally met because several topics that came up took time; however, we made progress as a group.

After the second meeting, I processed out with the facilitators and went to a therapist to do my own processing out. I headed home again for rest and relaxation and then went back to Memorial Sloan Kettering Cancer Center the next day to continue my reconstruction process. My personal journey at Sloan I did not share with the group.

As I mentioned a bit earlier, we allowed the group to share helpful information during our weekly meetings. Sometimes the information was about upcoming meetings for families of 9/11, and other times it was music, prose, poetry, or letters they had received over the week. One day, one of the mothers read a letter that she had received from Kathie Scobee-Fulgham, the daughter of Dick Scobee, commander of the Space Shuttle *Challenger*, on its final mission. I felt that Kathie's letter contained such a powerful message that I requested permission from Kathie to share it in this book. In this message, she explains how she felt after her dad died and talks about the feelings in her heart for the children of 9/11.

A LETTER TO THE YOUNGEST VICTIMS OF THE TERRORIST ATTACKS Of 9/11

With permission from Kathie Scobee-Fulgham

"Dear Children,

The thunderous explosions that rocked the whole world have shattered yours.

Why does the TV show the crashing plane, exploding and collapsing buildings over and over? Where is my mom or dad? Why can't the rescuers find him/her? Who could have done this terrible thing? Why is the whole nation crying?

Yours is a small voice in a crashing storm of questions arising from an act of war on the American people. But no answers will bring you comfort. And no answers will bring you closer to understanding, save one: Your mom or dad was in harm's way.

While our great nation bulks up for the first fight of the century, we the **Challenger** Children, and our nation mourn with you, for itself and for you. But yours is also a personal loss that is separate from this national tragedy. We hope this letter will bring you comfort, now or in the future, when you are strong enough – old enough – to read it.

We want to prepare you for what's to come and to help you deal with this burden you never asked to bear. No one asked the people in the World Trade Center, in the Pentagon, or on the airplanes to give their lives in a war they had never volunteered to fight, against people they did not even know were plotting their deaths. Your mom or dad was innocent. They were just doing their jobs or traveling to see friends or family, but someone decided to make their everyday lives – and yours – a battlefield.

You've discovered by now that you won't be able to escape the barrage of news, and the countless angles of investigation, speculation, and exasperation. The 24-hour coverage will ebb and flow but will blindside you in the weeks, months, and years to follow when you least expect it. You will be watching television and then, suddenly, there will be those pictures – the plane, the towers, the cloud of dust, the fires, and the people running.

For other people watching, this will all be something called "history." To you, it's your life. Just know the media and the public perception of this catastrophe aren't the same as yours. They can't know how painful it is to watch your mom or dad die several times each day. If they knew how much pain it caused, they would stop.

You imagine death like it is a fairytale or like at grandma and grandpa's funeral. They look peaceful in their coffins. Their earthly bodies are tangible and recognizable. You can say goodbye to someone who looks like your loved one. The physical proof – the recognizable person that was your mom or dad – is gone whole or not recognizable. Your mind can't accept it, even though your heart knows it. You know their spirit has gone to heaven, but it's hard to say goodbye. You will find your own way to say goodbye in your own time. All the children of public disasters are hearing your hearts break, holding your hands, and hugging you from afar. You are not alone. We want you to know that it will be bad – very bad – for a little while, but it will get better.

You see, 15 years ago, before some of you were even born, I watched my father and his crew die in a horrible accident. Our loved ones were astronauts on board the Space Shuttle **Challenger,** which blew up a few minutes after takeoff. It all happened on live television. It should have been a moment of private grief, but instead it turned into a very public torture. We couldn't turn on the television for weeks afterward, because we were afraid we would see the gruesome spectacle of the **Challenger** coming apart a mile up in the sky.

My father died a hundred times a day on televisions all across the country. And since it happened so publicly, everyone in the country felt like it happened to them, too, and it did. The **Challenger** explosion was a national tragedy. Everyone who saw it, everyone hurt, everyone grieved, everyone wanted to help, but that did not make it any easier for me. They wanted to say goodbye to American heroes. I just wanted to say goodbye to my daddy. You may feel sick when you think about his or her broken body. Your imagination might even carry you to new and scary depths and unspeakable images. You will be afraid to ask what happened because the answers might be worse than what you imagined. You'll worry yourself sick wondering if they felt pain, if they suffered, if they knew what was happening. They didn't. In the same way your brain doesn't register pain immediately when you break your arm, your mom or dad didn't know pain in their last moments of life on this earth.

You may have strange dreams or nightmares about your mom or dad being alive, trapped somehow, in a pocket of wreckage of the building or stranded or lost in some remote location after parachuting out of the plane before it crashed. They may call to you in your dream to come find them. You will wake up with such hope and determination, only to have clouds of reality gather and rain fresh tears of exasperation and sadness on your face.

These dreams are your subconscious-self trying to make sense out of what your conscious self already knows.

You will think about the last things you said to each other, were they loving words or actions? Did we speak sharply to each other? Were we too sleepy or rushed to even have one last look at each other's faces? Rest easy. Their last thoughts were of you, the all of who you are, not the Tuesday morning September 11, you. They were happy thoughts, all in a jumble of emotions so deep they are everlasting.

Everyone you know will cry fresh tears when they see you. People will try to feed you even though you know it all tastes like cardboard. They will want to know what you think – what you feel – what you need. But you really don't know. You may not know for a very long time. It will be even a longer time before you can imagine your life without mom or dad.

Some people, working through their own grief will want to talk to you about the catastrophe, the aftermath, the rescue, and the recovery, or the actions that will be taken by our nation. Others will whisper as you walk by "Her dad was killed in the attack on the World Trade Center" or "His mom was in the plane that crashed into the Pentagon" or "His dad was one of the firefighters who died when the buildings collapsed." This new identity might be difficult for you. Sometimes you will want to say to the whispers "Yes, that was my dad. We are so proud of him. I miss him like crazy!" Sometimes you will want to fade into the background, wanting to anonymously grieve in your own way, in your own time, without an audience.

When those who loved your mom or dad talk with you, cry with you, or even scream with frustration and unfairness of it, you don't have to make sense of it all.

Grief is a weird and winding path with no real destination and lots of switchbacks. Look on grief as a journey — full of rest stops, enlightening sites, and potholes of differing depths of rage, sadness, and despair. Just realize that you won't be staying forever at one stop. You will eventually move on to the next. And the path will become smoother, but it may never come to an end.

Ask the people who love you and who knew your mom or dad to help you to remember the way they lived – not the way they died. You need stories about your mom and dad from their friends, their co-workers, and your family. These stories will keep your mom or dad alive in your heart and mind for the rest of your life. Listen carefully to the stories. Tell them. Write them. Record them. Post them online. The stories will help you remember. The stories will help you make decisions about your life – help *you become the person you were meant to be. Just as a stronger nation will rise out of the grisly cinders and steel skeletal remains of buildings and airplanes, so will you be a stronger person. These events will shape your life in many different ways.*

You will wonder if you'll ever be safe again. You will. Our nation will wage a mighty war on terrorism. You will be protected. You can still believe in the future – in your future.

Please know that we are with you – holding you in our hearts, in our minds, and in all our prayers."

Kathie, thank you for these tender words from your heart, words that touched our children with compassion. You have made the world a better place not only in your name, but also in your brave and heroic father's name, Commander Richard Scobee. It is most appropriate to share your letter in this book. On January 28, 2019, our country marked the thirty-third anniversary of the Space Shuttle *Challenger* disaster. Kathie has served as a member of the advisory board for The *Challenger* Center for Space Science Education.

The mass grief and public trauma Kathie refers to in her letter only magnified the traumatic complicated grief reaction for the families of 9/11. Everywhere they went, photos could be seen of the burning towers, images that would last forever in their minds. It was deeply personal and so very private, yet television news shows led with coverage of the event for weeks and months. Magazines and newspapers ran stories on their front pages, over and over, and would do so on every anniversary. Everywhere our families went — grocery stores, drug stores, coffee shops — the pain would be there. One of the family members told me that even in her children's doctor's office, publications showing the burning towers sat on tables in the waiting room. The wound was constantly being opened.

How painful it must be for all of them, I thought. The grief process would be tedious for these families. It would mean more grief work needed to be done including a more extensive exploration of feelings. Being able to recognize these feelings, embrace them, and speak about them would be important. The familiar loved one who became the victim on 9/11 was part of a sudden unfamiliar life-ending disaster; they did not die in an intimate way with family around a bedside, but in a public murder shown on mass media. Most loved ones were unable to even say goodbye. All of it was acutely difficult for the bereaved to process through.

OCTOBER 14, 2001
SUNDAY: 9:30 a.m.
PIER 94 ~ NEW YORK CITY

Early on Sunday morning, I decided to put on my shoes and take action. With my husband Bob at my side, I journeyed into New York City to Pier 94 along the Hudson River. We parked on Fiftieth Street and began walking to the Family Center, located at Twelfth and Fifty-fourth Streets. The streets were empty as we walked toward the large, covered pier and continued on to the entrance of the facility.

All along the walkways, the Boy Scouts of America and Girl Scouts of America troops had left homemade cookies and brownies neatly wrapped in cellophane bags with brightly colored bows, perched carefully on the railings of the barriers. People had posted pictures of their lost loved ones at every turn.

We approached the doorway and were greeted by a welcoming, pleasant middle-aged woman. I explained why we were there, which was to aid the families of the victims of 9/11 at our support group in New Jersey. We were then passed on to a guide named Jennifer, who was most informative. I was so impressed.

Not many people were there to seek help. Maybe it was the time of day or they had come weeks earlier.

Lining the interior perimeter of the building were stations for government agencies, such as the Red Cross and FEMA. I spotted grief therapy dogs, a wall of teddy bears, and a wall of artwork and letters from children and schools all across the nation. Each company that had lost employees had a booth, including Cantor Fitzgerald, Marsh & McLennan, AON Corporation, and many others. There was also a cafeteria and a young children's play area.

I had discovered a source of knowledge so logically brought together in one place. After walking around and observing the setup, I knew that I needed to strongly encourage all of the families to come visit. For them, this place was at the heart of the matter. At the same time, I had to respect that for many of our families, a trip to New York might be too painful. I planned to charter a bus for everyone who wanted to visit Pier 94. I left the building with materials and information to pass out at our next meeting.

OCTOBER 16, 2001
TUESDAY: 10:30 a.m.
PAPERWORK

At the request of our families, we planned an extra meeting on a Tuesday to address the paperwork issue. A young lawyer and estate planner whom I had met at a neighborhood gathering offered his services, so I invited him to speak. While processing him in, I described what he would visibly experience and our code of confidentiality and then asked how he was feeling. He said that he felt good to be there. We proceeded into the room, and I quickly observed how overwhelming it was for him. Over time, I found that other speakers had a similar response. So much grief all in one place can do that to people. The families helped to make the young lawyer more comfortable, and he was able to give his talk. I think he was quite helpful for the group. We thanked him for his goodness and for sharing his gift with us. I processed him out, validated his feelings, and walked him to the door.

After returning to the room, I passed out the materials I had acquired on my trip to Pier 94. I strongly encouraged the families to pay a visit there and even offered to reserve a bus for them. I asked them to sign up, but no one did.

A young pregnant woman in the group seemed to be very knowledgeable on the paperwork issue. In a few weeks, she would be leaving the group to have her baby in Florida, where her parents could support her. Concerning paperwork, she suggested I contact a man at the United Way who had been so helpful to her. She thought that the man might be able to visit our group and bring some booklets to aid the families with the paperwork. I left the meeting and called him. He agreed to come. I scheduled him for the following week and gave him a time limit for speaking, something I was now doing with all of our guests.

OCTOBER 18, 2001
THURSDAY: 10:30 a.m.
HELPING "CHILDREN IN GRIEF"

We had a good turnout on this day and opened with the focus on "Children and Grief." Karen, our new children's group leader, explained the work she planned to do with the children and described the program as an "Expressive Arts Program" for children. The families asked lots of questions, and Karen answered them all. Her knowledge was invaluable to us.

I must share my feelings on children in our society experiencing loss of a loved one due to death and divorce. I have a dream that every child never grieves alone. I have a dream of bereavement education and art therapy in support group sessions being available to our kids after school in every school in the nation. I do recognize that schools have child psychologists and guidance counselors why not support groups? Those children might then have a "buddy" who is experiencing his or her loss and would recognize they are not alone. I believe we would see a difference on issues with drug, alcohol abuse, and numbers in suicide loss, maybe even a decrease in school shootings. We simply need to address loss in children. A Children's Place where children come to be with other children experiencing loss. What comes to mind is "Good Grief" now located in three areas of New Jersey and in Fort Meyers,

Florida, Valerie's House that is expanding. There are many places popping up over the country.

Our next presenter was a representative from Camp Comfort, an organization that helps aid children experiencing loss. Our volunteers, Marion Gaydos and Pat Lunny, had worked with the camp through their affiliation with Saint Mark Episcopal Church in Basking Ridge. This was the first of two meetings the camp would make a presentation and, later on in the year at another meeting, the founder of the camp would visit.

During the meeting, one of the participants asked me if the group could meet more often than once a week. I explained that doing so could be a disservice to the families and take away their time for living. The bereavement overload they were experiencing because of the traumatic complicated grief along with additional bereavement group meetings would be too heavy for them. I was cognizant that many group members were busy with their children plus our group.

One idea I suggested in lieu of additional group meetings was a "buddy" date, which could be another form of support for them. Coffee dates, playdates for the children, phone calls, etc. — it did not matter as long as they had someone they could plan a date with and maybe talk about their grief together. I asked that each one of them choose a "buddy" from the group to stay connected with. If they were connected to a person who had a similar loss, it might be helpful. (Some members had lost children, some lost spouses and siblings, and some lost fiancés.) I passed out cards for them to exchange their information and explained that buddies should meet each week or connect by phone. (In the weeks ahead, I noticed that the buddies became very close.)

Once again, I strongly encouraged the families to visit with a one-on-one therapist. I suggested that anyone who had not done so already should make at least one appointment and one for the children too (as many of the families were already doing). Therapists had been sending me their cards, but I could only refer for most of them and was unable to recommend because I did not know many of the therapists personally. I asked the therapists who contacted me to give the families three free sessions to discern whether the therapist might be a good match for them, and all of the therapists complied.

Because our group continued to grow with each meeting (we had thirty-five at this meeting), I found myself constantly repeating tools and actions for healing. I would suggest, go and see an uplifting movie, take time to exercise, go for walks, listen to soft music, get a massage, attend yoga classes, enjoy a bike ride, eat well and drink plenty of water. These are all good tools during this time. I repeated once again that traumatic complicated grief was bereavement overload, as it truly was. I wanted them to stay as balanced as possible and not add to the overload by scheduling additional meetings. However, as time past several additional meetings were warranted.

I realized that this was a good time to look at "Positive and Negative Coping Mechanisms." Those things that I had just suggested to the group, such as exercising, listening to soft music, journaling, and meditation, and joining a support group, were all positive coping mechanisms. However, I stressed that any one thing done in excess can throw a person off balance. I then talked about negative coping mechanisms, such as alcohol and drug abuse, as well as isolation and extremes in eating, working, and exercise. Those things could compound the loss. The goal is to stay as balanced as possible.

We then reviewed the *Five Stages of Grief* that we had learned in a previous meeting. My goal was to break down into small groups. The plan was for the small groups to springboard off a question. What stage of grief did you experience today? Was it denial, bargaining, anger, depression, or acceptance? Do you ever find yourself stuck in any one stage? The group did try small groups, and lots of dialogue could be heard. However, we did hear feedback they liked being together in the larger group better.

OCTOBER 25, 2001
THURSDAY: 10:30 a.m.
(40 in attendance) - We continue to grow.
PAPERWORK

Three representatives from the United Way attended today's meeting. They passed out informational forms and offered the group some guidance. This meeting was complicated because the families were all from different towns and districts. We had people attending from Long Island, Hoboken, and Jersey City, along with other tri-state locales. Our families from Basking Ridge were being serviced under Catholic Charities and the United Way was helping in other areas. I realized that my planning should have been more thorough and that the large group should have been broken up into smaller groups based on locales. I suggested that the participants engage privately in their own towns. I do think the positive that came out of this day was that some of the people who had not thought about doing paperwork started to. Unfortunately, the meeting was difficult for me because I had to cut the program I had planned.

Jean, a generous and kind lady and a friend of one of our group members, donated beautiful knit flag scarves in red, white, and blue to all of the members of our group. The scarves really made a hit, and we wore them everywhere we went. Thank you, Jean, for your goodness! The scarves kept us warm all winter long; we just loved them!

After the meeting was over, one of the group members, a young pregnant mom named Katy, asked me if I might have time to work with her four boys for an hour during the week. I agreed, and we planned a "getting to know you visit" for early the next week at their Basking Ridge home. Walking into their home, I was welcomed with a warm embrace from Katy. However, it was a one-armed hug, for in her other arm she held a bouncing blonde, curly-haired, blue-eyed, nineteen-month-old baby girl who smiled shyly with her angelic face. I was escorted into the large family room where I sat and was offered a cold drink. The baby wiggled out of her mother's arms and tottered over to pick up a toy.

I instantly observed a busy day, indeed, in this household. Then again, I thought, it must always be a busy day, only more magnified now since the death of a dearly beloved man who had lived here weeks earlier. I observed kids coming and going, being dropped off by friends from sports practices and playdates. I noticed the boys were lingering in the driveway with neighborhood kids. I was introduced to kind neighbors stopping in with dinner for the night. The phone was ringing nonstop. Everyone was reaching out to help this family.

I conversed with Katy for a while in order to learn more about the support systems she had surrounding her. I told her I could get more help for her if she needed.

The children came breezing into the house intermittently, and their mom introduced each one to me. There were four adorable sandy-haired boys, young and vivacious, one in every size. I admired the pictures on the tables and walls that painted a vision in my mind of a loving, beautiful family of great promise. The children resembled their handsome dad, who had been described to me as a man of strength and a vital member of their family, one they would sorely miss with the many questions in their minds of how to go forward without him. I said my goodbyes and returned home to plan my next visit with the children.

I started out my second visit with supplies for the children to make memory boxes. I quickly realized that artwork meetings would go only so far! On the following visit, I took the boys into a field at the local park. I gave them each a brown cardboard box and asked them to write on the box the name of something they wanted to kick. All of them picked the same name that I had chosen to put on my box. Can you guess that name? From the large box of crayons I had brought with me, I told them to pick any color crayon to write with. Black and red were the colors of choice. Even the second-grader knew just how to spell the name, and he scribbled it recklessly on the box. I then took them to a soccer field and asked them to kick their boxes from one goal to the other. I followed along behind them. The boxes ended up in tatters. I told them they could put the boxes in the dumpster or keep them. Two of the boys kept them. Since the developmental stages were varied, I could see that journaling and drawing might be another way to help the boys.

On my next visit, I gave each of the boys a journal. I told them to keep the journal next to their beds, and each day they could write down their feelings or draw pictures of just a round face with how they were feeling. It could be a face that was happy, sad, or mad for that day. I suggested, too, that they could jot down just one word a day and draw a picture for that word, if they chose to. On another visit, I used clay with them to form symbols of who their dad was for them. They seemed to really like this exercise.

I made five visits to their home over a five-week period and then I suggested to Katy that it would be beneficial for the boys to have some one-on-one sessions with a childhood therapist. I also told her about our children's group that would be starting up at the church. I mentioned a couple of other things that might be helpful for the boys, such as sports programs and maybe a new pet further down the road since their family dog had died shortly before their father. Katy graciously agreed to pursue these avenues. From time to time, I stopped by for a friendly visit in their home.

REFLECTIONS FROM JULIE LEE, CHLIDCARE VOLUNTEER

My work with The Saint James 9/11 Bereavement Support Group was one of the most moving experiences of my life. When I was asked if I wanted to join the effort, I knew I wanted to be a part of helping the families as best I could. We all felt so helpless and deeply troubled by 9/11, but this was something concrete we could do.

We had very constructive planning meetings with the team where the tasks were laid out before us and duties assigned. I thought the program was very well organized. The most important task was planning the actual weekly bereavement programs for the group, including music, poetry, candle lightings, writing messages to the deceased loved ones, and so much more. Other tasks were shopping for supplies, babysitting the young children during the meetings, organizing donations of snacks and lunches for the meetings from local restaurants, and starting a library of consoling books about grief.

Walking into the church meeting room on the first day was almost overwhelming. The sense of loss and profound grief and fear among the families, so many of them women who were in their twenties and thirties with young children, was very heavy. It was hard to find words to communicate our deep sympathy to the families, but one thing we could do was go to work.

My main duty was babysitting the infants and young children who came with their mothers. These children were so young that they could not understand what had happened to their fathers. I marveled that the young mothers could carry on caring for these young ones, while still trying to deal with the shock of their husbands' disappearances and deaths. It seemed doubly cruel that they did not even have a body to grieve over. The circumstances of their husbands' deaths were so awful. I think many of them continued to wonder what their husbands' last moments were like.

I was not in the main meeting room where the group meetings were held, as I was in a separate babysitting room. I think all of us volunteers felt that the main meeting room was sacred ground. God was working in there, giving the grief facilitators the right words, and beginning to help the families to help each other to find a way forward.

Week after week, the group met. There was a consoling theme every week, beautiful music, special guests, and special gifts from companies like Bobbi Brown Cosmetics and "The Bear Makin' Ladies" with their handmade teddy bears, and from groups in our town and from around the country. The families were always treated with gentleness and the utmost respect. I came to admire these young families tremendously. They appreciated everything we did. At the beginning, they could hardly speak, and there was so much profound grief. I came to see that over time they seemed to grow stronger and to take on tasks for which many of the widows used to depend on their husbands. Some of these tasks were driving great distances at holidays with their children to visit relatives, planning vacations for themselves and their children, organizing repairs to their homes, all while dealing with their own and their children's grief. Seeing them managing well, by necessity, gave me more courage to live my own life, I think. I realized that I could do more than I used to think I could.

Overall, it was a life-changing experience to help the families. I hope we were able to give them some hope and comfort at that terrible time.

November: Anger and Holiday Preparations

NOVEMBER 1, 2001
THURSDAY: 10:30 a.m.
42 - in attendance
ANGER

I invited a therapist friend of mine, Sister Catherine Morrisatt from Grace Counseling in Madison, New Jersey, to help us address Anger. She had spoken at other groups that I had run in the past, and I liked working with her. I knew she would be a good choice for this meeting. I greeted her warmly, and she explained her program. I am indebted to Sister Catherine for her support to me during 9/11 and the many other times in life when she stood by me.

Anger can play a big part in any grief process, but for our group, anger was front and center because of the traumatic complicated grief, caused by murder and sudden death, one that could have been avoided many thought, and the media constantly reopening the wounds. Anger was an emotion the survivors had to confront.

After Sister Catherine gave her presentation on dealing with anger, I told the group that I would speak on Constructive versus Destructive Anger the following week. I chose kickboxing as an example of a constructive method to release the anger. A local kickboxing business offered to come work with the group, and I told everyone to come in comfortable clothing for the exercise on the following Tuesday. I also addressed destructive anger, which may arise in relationships with others, be it with family or friends or possibly in the workplace. It is better to secure and protect those relationships and to work on the anger in a constructive way. It is not appropriate to take your anger out on people. The anger can be released at a real gym with real punching bags or through tennis, golf, or whatever avenue a person chooses. There are better ways to deal with anger than taking it out on someone else. I used to tell clients to use a pillow if they couldn't find a punching bag.

Next, I talked about one of my teachers, Dr. Kenneth Doka, PhD, and his theories on **Disenfranchised Grief**. This kind of loss is not openly acknowledged, socially validated by others, or publicly observed. It is a hidden sorrow. I brought this topic up because our group had five fiancés, and the loss was so very hard for them. All of their hopes and dreams were lost suddenly on 9/11. Their wedding dates would be coming up, and they would be alone. The victims' families would be responsible for planning their memorials, hopefully including the fiancés in the planning and offering to include them to play a role in the funeral ritual if they wished. I have dealt with individuals who felt feelings of heavy helplessness and hopelessness at a time like this and feelings of hidden sorrow. This may not be true in all cases. I can remember another case about a fiancé who lost her loved one in a plane crash. Only the immediate family members were allowed to go to meetings with the airlines concerning the crash. The feelings of isolation and not being included resulted in hidden sorrow. I would hope this would not be true in today's world since that case happened early on in my work. The 9/11 fiancés stayed with us in our support group for only a couple of months; they were mostly young professionals who needed to go back to work not having much time off to grieve. I suggested they form their own group at night and invite speakers, and they did. I made a note to keep them informed of speakers we would have at our group gatherings in case any of the fiancés wanted to attend. We did see their faces from time to time anyway.

As the meeting wound down, I urged our group to attend the "Mass of Remembrance" to be celebrated at the church the following night on the Feast of All Souls. We ended our meeting with a ritual remembering all those who died, and we lit candles and sprinkled in prayerful music. Ritual always proves to be a positive coping mechanism during the bereavement process, and I used it often.

NOVEMBER 2, 2001
FRIDAY: 7:00 p.m.
THE MASS OF REMEMBRANCE
LOCATION: SAINT JAMES CHURCH

This evening was a sad but beautiful celebration of the lives of loved ones who had died this past year, not just on 9/11. I had asked my friend Steve Kirbos, an outstanding singer who had supported me with the bereaved in the past, to join us. Steve was from the Metuchen Diocese in New Brunswick, New Jersey. With his soothing voice, he would enrich the atmosphere I had envisioned for this mass. Monsignor was the celebrant, and I was the lector.

As the families entered the back of the church, Elise and the other facilitators guided them to write the names of their loved ones who had died in the *Book of the Deceased* on the podium in the center aisle. The families were then asked to bring flowers they had been given to the vase in front of the altar when their loved ones' names were read out loud during the mass. One of our families brought up the gifts of bread and wine along with the *Book of the Deceased* during the offertory. This was a touching evening of remembrance, and Monsignor eloquently delivered a powerful homily.

NOVEMBER 6, 2001
TUESDAY: 10:30 a.m.
Twenty In attendance
KICKBOXING

Kickboxing instructors, come right in! This was part of my plan to help group members deal with their anger in a constructive way. I attached pictures onto the pads of whom I thought they might want to kick. Can you guess whom? I sensed that participants found it beneficial. Several weeks later, we were invited to visit the kickboxing facility for another session. Many in the group liked it so much that they signed up for a membership!

NOVEMBER 8, 2001
THURSDAY: 10:30 a.m.
(45 in attendance)
SURVIVOR FAMILIES OF PAST TERRORIST ATTACKS

While ministering to previous groups, I had invited my friend, Stephen Flatow, to speak one of the times. He and his wife lived in West Orange, New Jersey, and they had lost their beautiful daughter, Alisa on April 10, 1995, while she was participating in a Jewish-American study Program in Isreal. Alisa, age 20, was killed in a suicide bombing attack on a bus carried out by militants belonging to the Islamic Jihad Movement in Palestine. Stephen has made incredible strides in his quest for justice in his beloved daughter's name. He is a motivational and an inspirational individual; it is truly an honor to know the story of his heart. What he has accomplished in life is phenomenal and unimaginable.

Knowing how passionate Stephen is and how much insight he could give to the families, I invited him to speak at this meeting. After I warmly introduced Stephen, he explained how he had lost his daughter and the difficult road of grief that he and his family had traveled on since. He described how he went on to form a foundation in Alisa's name, keeping alive memories of her. He told about how each member of his family dealt differently with the loss. Recognizing that members of our group were working through similar feelings, he assured them they would go forward as he had. This is exactly what I wanted the group to hear.

When Stephen finished, I introduced a second speaker named Kathy Tedeschi, a woman from southern New Jersey whose husband died in *Pan Am flight 103*. This was the first time I met Kathy. I read a quote from her in the newspaper and tracked her down. Kathy talked about her husband, Bill, who died over Lockerbie, Scotland, when the plane he was traveling on crashed on December 21, 1988. Kathy discussed her difficult experience as a single mom and dealing with her children. She also told about her loss and how it affected her and her family. She concluded by talking about her role in pursuing legal actions against Pan American Airlines, which resulted in the airline closing down.

The group was full of questions for Stephen and Kathy. Both swiftly connected to the group. They were inspirational and effective witnesses of survivorship. After their loved ones' horrific deaths, these two were still living and living in positive transformative ways. According to the feedback, this program was helpful for all in attendance.

My neighbors, Sue and Vince Walls, generously donated patriotic gifts to the group. Everyone received a t-shirt that read "United We Stand" in bold red, white, and blue letters. We all put the t-shirts on and had a group photo taken with Stephen and Kathy.

Our next meeting would be our last meeting before the Thanksgiving holiday. Families would be spending their first major holiday without their loved ones, so I wanted to give them the necessary coping skills as well as a lasting memory in honor of their loved ones. My team and I decided on a balloon launch for the first part of the program.

Even though a balloon launch sounds simple, lots of thought goes into this kind of an event. Since timing was important, I first called the nearby Morristown Airport, and the flight control people directed me to call them twenty minutes before we released the balloons. Two days before our planned balloon launch, *American Airlines Flight 587* went down over a neighborhood in Queens, New York. You can believe I was going to follow the instructions given by the airport personnel!

NOVEMBER 15, 2001
THURSDAY: 10:30 a.m.
45 - in attendance
BALLOON LAUNCH AND "DEALING WITH THE HOLIDAYS"

Our meeting opened with a scripture reading:

> "We do not want you to be unaware, brothers and sisters, about those who have fallen asleep, so that you may not grieve like the rest, who have no hope."
> (1 Thess. 4:13)

Soothing prayerful music filled the room as I handed each person in the group a purple heart to honor their loved one as a hero. The heart was made of paper with a hole in the corner, and I asked them to write a Thanksgiving message or a letter they would have written to their loved one before that loved one died. As the music continued to play, I lowered the lighting and left the room, hearing sniffles. This was a very hard exercise for everyone. I returned ten minutes later and asked the group to tie their hearts on to biodegradable green balloons with yellow ribbons. I like to symbolize ritual with color, green being the color for hope and yellow the color for resurrection.

We filed out into the field behind the church. The day was cool with the sun moving in and out of the clouds. I read a letter to them from their deceased loved ones, a letter I had used often in these rituals, touching their hearts and souls. Then I put on a moving song by Paul Alexander entitled "Pretty Balloon." Next, I asked the group to release the balloons into the blue and white sky. Many tears were shed on this sad occasion. All remarked that a bird flew high above through the balloons as they floated up to the heavens. Slowly, we walked back into the building.

Dr. Eileen Kohutis, PhD, a therapist, met us in the room to talk about "Dealing with the Holidays." The facilitators handed out rolled up red and green papers tied with ribbons. These pages were filled with tips to help the families deal with the upcoming holiday.

Elise handed out eight-day candles she obtained from Cookie Dolan, one of our parishioners, who often and so generously supplied us with candles. The families could light them and place them in front of their loved ones' pictures at home for the Thanksgiving weekend. I handed out a prayer for them to read at Thanksgiving dinner that included the deceased's name. I mentioned that they might ask their children to help plan the day with them. Some ideas I suggested were including prayer or a ritual, such as maybe planting a tree or raising a glass to toast the deceased loved one who has died. Telling past stories about them. Reminiscing around the dinner table can be helpful during that first year, while taking into consideration each family member, since all grieve differently. Or maybe even a trip away and doing something altogether different would be another plan to get through the day.

The meeting lasted nearly four hours, about our average length. The group voted to have a meeting on Tuesday the week after Thanksgiving. They did not feel they could wait until that Thursday, which would be a full two weeks since our last meeting. We concluded our time together with prayer.

NOVEMBER 27, 2001
TUESDAY: 10:30 a.m.
40 in attendance:
WHAT WAS THANKSGIVING LIKE/ BLESSING & DEDICATION OF "THE TREE OF MEMORY"

Moving this meeting to Tuesday was a good plan because the day was overflowing with grief work, and the families benefited from being in the room together.

Our meeting room was aglow with candles, and soft music played in the background. The Floral Committee had placed red poinsettias, donated by Berkeley Florist, on every seat. Next to the poinsettias were decorative bags containing nail and hair gift certificates from local establishments and coordinated by our Pampering Committee.

A lovely lady from Basking Ridge named Karen, called and told me she was a representative for Doctor Hauschka Beauty and Spa product line. She offered a complimentary foot massage and a facial, a combined three-hour treatment, for anyone in our group. When Karen said I should come first to experience the procedure, I hesitated, wondering how I could free up three hours. Reluctantly, I agreed. It was the best three-hour treatment of relaxation I had ever had, and I just loved it! Karen was right — it was well worth the time! At this particular meeting, I told the group about my experience and encouraged them to sign up. Several of the girls made appointments and came back later with positive remarks.

One of our parishioners at Saint James Church was a guy named Tom Gallo. He was the owner of Country Mile Gardens in Morristown, New Jersey. I had approached Tom to see if he might donate a "live" Christmas tree to our group. Big-hearted man that he is, Tom eagerly replied "Yes!" Monsignor gave us permission to plant the five-foot tree by the door of the new Parish Center where the families entered each week. Elise had a bronze plaque made to place in front of the tree. She had also made arrangements for a few men from the church to dig the hole prior to our meeting. We invited Monsignor to dedicate the tree with a blessing ceremony.

We all huddled in a tight circle around the tree on this rainy, cold, and dismal Tuesday morning. The volunteers had umbrellas to cover over us; they always thought of everything. After Monsignor blessed the tree, a volunteer lit the tree. "The Tree of Memory," inspirational music by Paul Alexander, played as each person took turns planting the ball of the tree and shoveling the dirt high around it. We then hung angel ornaments, each inscribed with a name of the deceased, on the boughs of the tree.

What a powerful, heartfelt ritual this was. We held close to one another. There were lots of tears. I could only liken it to shattered pieces all around me.

I had contacted the music department at Ridge High School and asked if violinists from the music department could play for us on this day. Stepping back into the building after the Christmas tree blessing ceremony, we were met by three teenage girls in lovely black dresses, playing "Silent Night" on their violins. An immediate feeling of soothing warmth came over our bodies and souls. Lights were low. The volunteers and musicians created an atmosphere of peacefulness and tranquility. It felt as though a soft blanket of angora was laid over us, giving us an inner feeling of comfort. It was oh so evident on this damp and dreary day.

Upon entering our room, we discovered that Elise had gifted us with a surprise of a 9/11 Christmas tree. It was artfully decorated and lit with an abundance of white lights. Sparkling balls of red, white, and blue along with beautiful flowers with ribbons and flags adorned the tree. It was just astonishingly beautiful. Elise was a gift to all of us.

The families traded paperwork, and great ideas were exchanged on this day. We watched a calming video from Willowgreen, Inc. on the bereavement process by one of my favorite healers, Dr. James Miller. He uses nature to aid those grieving. It had a good response and triggered dialogue.

Our educational piece on this day was a discussion on "Choices Made in the Grief Process." This issue is important to consider, for not all people will be the same. We can choose to let the loss deplete us, or we can go back to the way we were living, or we can climb to a higher plateau of living. The final option was my hope for each and every one in our group, I said.

The Madison Hotel continued to nourish us each week, and we ended the day with lunch together.

Observation: Lots of good grief work was accomplished today. This was a group of bright and educated individuals who were eager to do all they could to aid themselves and their families. They were good listeners and were openly expressive with each other in the group. They were just trying to stay afloat.

December: Preparing for Christmas

DECEMBER 6, 2001
THURSDAY: 10:30 a.m.
THE POTTER AND THE SINGER

A prayerful yet stimulating day was planned, to ease everyone's spirits.

Upon entering the room, members found on their seats, Girl Scouts Cookies sent by a local Girl Scout troop.

A German tradition that I handed down in my own family was to fill our children's Christmas stockings with sweets, fruit, and nuts on December 6. I decided to share the tradition with the group on this special Feast Day of Saint Nicholas. A generous gift of Cadbury Fruit and Nut candy bars also waited on each seat, courtesy of Kings Supermarket in neighboring Bernardsville, New Jersey. Accompanying the fruit and nut candy bars was an informative book on grief obtained by our librarian, Betsy.

Combined with soothing music led by my friend once again, Steve Kirbos from the Metuchen Diocese, our meeting for this day proved to be most moving. I was hoping to palliate the spirits of the grievers at this meeting, and I asked Monsignor to join us for the special program.

One of my favorite presenters, who had attended a couple of my other groups, is a potter named Ray Boswell from Sugar Loaf, New

York. Dressed in simple work clothes and adorned with his potter's apron, this kind man with dark brown hair and beard, maybe in his early 50's and slight in stature, was filled with the conviction of his faith in the living God. Ray guided us on a powerful journey into his "hands-on-art," pleasing to our eyes. He taught us lessons about life and death along the way as he made a chalice and a bowl for our group to use during future memorial services. We were mesmerized as he formed a cup into a beautiful chalice using only his fingertips. His message, delivered while he spun the wheel, was to stay centered on God. The group saw that when the pottery vessel was not centered, it would cave in around the edges.

Ray chose Terry, one of our girls in the group, to help make one of the vessels. She was a little shy at first, but then really got into making the pottery.

It was such a memorable day and well received. Good grief work that captured everyone's full attention happened.

DECEMBER 13, 2001
THURSDAY: 10:30
FOUR GRIEF TASKS of MOURNING and THE 6 R's PROCESSES

Today's meeting began with scripture,

> "My soul rests in God alone from whom comes my salvation. God alone is my rock, and my salvation."
> (Ps. 62:1)

I launched into the program. On display in front of the room, were two large white foam boards with bold black letters describing two theories for healing yourself through the grief process.

J. William Worden, PhD, ABPP author of *Grief Counseling and Grief Therapy: A Handbook for the Mental Health Practitioner,* 4th *edition,* a clinical psychologist, and a member of American Board of

Professional Psychology, wrote the *Four Tasks of Mourning* theory. The tasks are:

- First Task: To Accept the Reality of the Loss
- Second Task: To Process the Pain of Grief
- Third Task: To Adjust to a World without the Deceased
- Fourth Task: To Find an Enduring Connection with the Deceased in the Midst of Embarking on a New Life

After some discussion, I then moved to the other large presentation board. This one illustrated a stage model devised by Dr. Therese Rando, PhD, BCBT, a clinical psychologist, a thanatologist, a traumatologist, and author of *Treatment of Complicated Mourning*.

I delved into complicated grief reaction that I said was due to a traumatic death and also resulting from the mode of death being murder, a sudden death that was unanticipated, and for lack of a body to ritualize or even visualize. To complicate it even more, it was a mass and public death heightened by the media. The traumatic complicated grief can be described as an abnormal grief that can result in complete loss of previous positive beliefs or worldview. It is also bereavement overload with many feelings darting all around. I thought there might be some in our group still waiting for the loved one to walk through the door. I must note that both of these two theories by Worden and Rando could be applied to the complicated grief process. I made it known to the group that the process involved great pain and emotional adjustment and was a process that in both cases would take a longer time while adjusting to this significant loss of their beautiful loved one in their lives.

Dr. Rando's theory is as follows:

The Six R's Processes are preceded by Phases:
Avoidance Phase
1. Recognize the loss

Confrontation Phase
2. React to the separation
3. Recollect and re-experience
Accommodation Phase
4. Relinquish old attachments
5. Readjust and adopt new ways of being in the world
6. Reinvest emotional energy into new people in your life

I noted for the group that the constant media coverage would be something they would have to deal with in the years ahead of them. I observed that the reality of the loss was not yet there at this time. On a positive note, I observed, too, that they were confronting their grief, finding common ground within the group, though unique each unto themselves.

On this same day, it was important for me to help the group acknowledge the goodness that had come our way. We began by recognizing the Keller family, owners of The Madison Hotel and well-known individuals in the Morris County area. It was time to thank the entire family for their phenomenal gift of nourishing us during these difficult days, a period that had now stretched over two months. I invited Richard, their liaison, into the meeting room along with Monsignor and Chris and Angel, our hospitality chairpersons. A group member delivered a commendation, and Chris and Angel presented an engraved Golden Eagle plaque honoring the Keller family for their long-term aid to our group.

Another plaque that we awarded on this day was to the Hilliard Farber Securities Corporation. Their offices were situated across the street from the World Trade Center. Through the joint efforts of one of their employees, Jerry Galgano, who was also a parishioner of Saint James Church, many families in need were helped, and we were enabled to produce the programs that we knew could most benefit the families.

We were enormously grateful to both of these businesses for their outreach and support in meeting the needs of the 9/11 families. We will never forget their goodness.

A few weeks earlier, I had driven into New York City to attend my husband's company Christmas party. The event was to be held at a restaurant near the World Trade Center, our small way of supporting the area. The night was dark and foggy, somewhat eerie, I recall. My cell phone rang, on our car ride into NYC and I answered to hear the sweet voice of a woman on the other end. She said she was calling on behalf of 20/20, a women's group in Birmingham, Alabama. She told me that her group had read about us and wanted to send handmade bracelets to each member of our group. How kind, I thought, and what goodness bearing light in the darkness at an unexpected time. I just marveled at the call as we parked the car.

The bracelets were received a week later and distributed at this meeting. They were made of attractive red, white, and blue stones, with silver charms of hearts, crosses, and Bibles attached. They were made with loving care, and beautiful treasures indeed! We all took delight in marveling at them. How grateful we felt! A kind note was attached from these loving and compassionate souls:

Dear Precious Ladies,

I am from Birmingham, Alabama. I just wanted to write you and let you know that even though I don't know you, my thoughts and prayers are with you. When we feel lost, we can go to the Bible or to God in prayer and He will show us the way. Think of this when you see the Bible on your bracelet. When you look at the cross, think of God's unconditional love. He loved us so much that He sent His only Son Jesus to die on the cross for remission of our sins (John 3:16). When you look at the heart, you can think about compassion and how much we feel for you and your loss.

Take care and God bless you,
Renee R.

I had asked Monsignor to give the group a "Christmas Blessing" to conclude the meeting. There were few dry eyes on this day.

DECEMBER 14, 2001
FRIDAY: 10:30 a.m.
CHRISTMAS "THANK YOU" LUNCHEON TO VOLUNTEERS

Our volunteers continued to provide invaluable aid. I had such gladness in my heart for each and every one of them. Affirmation for their goodness was imperative. I planned a Christmas luncheon at my home and invited several of the group to help serve. I also invited Santa Claus and his helper, Mrs. Claus, who handed out little angel ornaments, a symbol for "The Angel Hands Group." The Clauses brought smiles to our faces as they invited each of the volunteers to sit on Santa's lap, and Santa consoled many of them. It was a beautiful sight to behold.

Pat and Camille Ficcio, our Santa and Mrs. Claus, were friends of mine from earlier days working at St. Patrick Church in Chatham, New Jersey. Pat's first wife, Claire, who had been a hospice patient of mine, had died several years earlier. Pat had re-married a lovely woman, Camille, a few years later. I was honored to be present at their wedding. Pat and Camille were both truly a loving and connected couple. They will always occupy a warm spot in my heart! Through this event, Pat was able to bring Christmas to others and transform his own grief. It was an uplifting day for all of us.

The goodness of our volunteers, now sixty-eight men and women strong, was ever present. When they took action, it was straight from their hearts. They did everything in the most thoughtful ways, with a twist of love at every step. They just amazed me each week with their ingenuity. They were talented, creative, compassionate, and loving individuals, shining examples of unconditional love for their fellow human beings. What a great group of people who put the wind in my sails every day I spent with them.

DECEMBER 20, 2001
THURSDAY: 10:30 a.m.
SHORT HILLS HILTON

Our group was invited to the Short Hills Hilton in nearby Short Hills, New Jersey, for a day of relaxation, which included a yoga class and foot massage plus a lovely lunch provided by Coldwell Banker. Only a small number attended the yoga and massage, but many more came for the lunch. I wrote a Christmas/holiday blessing and read it to the group before lunch. The day was a gift to help us through the holiday season.

The Rocky Grove Presbyterian Church in Franklin, Pennsylvania, sent big boxes of stuffed toys for our children's group. On December 16, 2001 the church had held its youth Christmas program. At the event, the children decided to send their collection of stuffed animals to the children of 9/11. The gifts were an unexpected surprise, one that was so greatly appreciated.

Carol W. sent a letter to our church from the community of Palmersville, Tennessee, a small town in the rural northwest corner of the state. Along with the letter, she sent us a large box of teddy bears, "filled with our thoughts, prayers, and hugs," she wrote. Carol stated in her letter, the bears and financial donations, were given by the Palmersville School Children, Larry's Gas Station, the Store, as well as the Weakley County Bank and the Woodmen of the World Life Insurance Company. Carol ended her letter by writing that she hoped to help make our new friends feel better. We were so touched by their support and certainly most grateful. People from around the country reached out to us. The goodness spread from afar.

DECEMBER 27, 2001
THURSDAY: 10:30 a.m.
(55 in attendance)

The group voted to meet on this day. They felt it was imperative to be together. I told the volunteers to take the day off, but they were there with lunch for all. Angel and Chris, our Hospitality Committee leaders, were exceptional!

The group then shared stories of how Christmas went. They expressed that they loved our program and could not live without it. We must have been doing something right, I thought!

Our numbers had increased to fifty-five adults and seventy-nine children with a parent lost on 9/11.

On this day the Avon Corporation, through the efforts of a member of our group, gave each child a nice monetary gift for the holidays. The money was raised from a "heart pin" sale, that Avon held over the holidays in efforts to raise support for the 9/11 families. We expressed warm Christmas/holiday wishes to the Avon Corporation and overflowing thanksgiving. This company certainly turned on our heart lights!

REFLECTIONS FROM CHRIS GREEN AND ANGEL HAND, HOSPITALITY

We can't express to you how much we wish there was no need for the bereavement group, that September 11th never happened, that you didn't lose someone so close to you. Many of us volunteers lost someone we loved and respected too, or just saw the pain and suffering everywhere we turned.

We were more saddened when we thought there was nothing we could do to help. Then Pam invited us to participate, in a small way, on your journey from grief into hope.

We've seen heartbroken spouses, sisters, mothers, and fiancés take many steps along that journey. That has helped us heal as well. Again, we are grateful to have helped in any way.

January: Beginning a New Year

JANUARY 3, 2002
THURSDAY: 10:30 a.m.

As I entered the room on this new day of 2002, champagne glasses filled with sparkling cider came into view. I began the meeting with a warm New Year's welcome and prayer, as well as a toast to hope, healing, renewal, and good health.

The group presented me with a silver frame engraved with a beautiful expression of their gratefulness. As they read it to me, tears fell from my eyes. I graciously accepted it on behalf of all our team, for we were one in this effort. I told the group that they were doing all the work healing each other and that we were just there to turn the lights on.

Personally, at this moment, I recall thinking that there was life after breast cancer, even though early on at times I had questioned if life could go on. I think I found that renewed sense of life through turning the lights on for the people in darkness, as well as through spreading God's message of hope to others. The 9/11 families were not only healing each other, but they were healing me at the same time, and they did not know it. It was their despair that gave me a reason for being and a purpose for living. Amazingly, on many days, I forgot that I had even had breast cancer.

Maureen Halley, our deacon's wife, visited on this day to explain "Healing Touch," an alternative relaxation therapy, to help aid our group. She extended her gift of goodness to our members with more visits over the next two weeks. She was food for our bodies and calmed our spirits during the trying days.

For the 2001 holiday season, red, white, and blue bulbs had adorned the Rockefeller Christmas Tree. The light bulbs were sent to us in small cellophane bags as a special gift for the families. We handed them out during the meeting to everyone as a keepsake.

MID-JANUARY MEETINGS

By January, our meetings had settled into a routine. The meetings opened with candle lightings, music, prayer, and inspirational thoughts. At the beginning of one meeting, the facilitators anointed the group members with the symbol of oil and a blessing to give them strength through the Spirit of God.

Group members continued to share information with each other. The influx of poems, essays, and emails was constant. One of the group members brought in a reading entitled *Meet Me in the Stairwell* by Stacey Randall. It was a sad and moving way to close that particular meeting.

Early on when the group had just started, I met a lot of resistance when I suggested breaking down into small groups for our discussion time. Because we had grown significantly and were averaging about sixty people per meeting, I knew we needed the intimacy of small groups. I thought the groups would not only create a more intimate setting, but also lead to free expression, and that proved to be the case when I again suggested small groups at our January 10th meeting. That day, the discussion question was, "what do you want out of life?" I instructed the individuals to give a one-word answer only. Within the small groups, they made a plan of action to attain this word as a group. At another meeting, I asked, "Have you ever been stuck in a stage of grief?" Our groups explored how we could develop a plan of action to help ourselves from becoming stuck.

Other notable gifts I received for the group during this time was an envelope of small crosses and Stars of David made from the outer covering of the tree beams of the World Trade Center building. These small treasures were gifts from a friend, George Travastino, a caring man whose heart was with the families of the disaster. They were given to him anonymously for the children of 9/11.

JANUARY 29, 2002
TUESDAY: 9 a.m.
THE STATE OF THE UNION ADDRESS: WASHINGTON, DC

Today, I accompanied our group's spokeswoman Katy, by train to Washington, DC. Katy, had been invited by Senator Jon Corzine of New Jersey to be his guest at the "State of the Union Address." This would be the first "State of the Union Address" given by President George W. Bush since he had taken office and four months since the September 11th attacks. (President Bush's speech from February 2001 is not considered an official State of the Union, but rather an "Address before a Joint Session of Congress.")

Katy was an attractive, young, Irish blonde, and a sweet mother of five children. Her mother had stepped in to watch the children at home in Basking Ridge while Katy made the trip. I did not approve of Katy traveling alone on the train since she was eight months pregnant with her sixth child, so I accompanied her.

While sitting on the train, I helped Katy open a stack of letters her family had received from all over the country. Katy shared with me so many beautiful and touching letters of condolences, from schools, Girl Scout Troops, and others. It was a very emotional time for her, but she read each and every one of them and wrote thank you notes back to the caring individuals as we traveled on the Acela Express to our nation's capital.

I was so pleased to know this mom. As a group, we had voted for her to be our spokesperson. I think we all recognized early on her outstanding qualities as a speechwriter, as well as a representative for us. She had been most impressive when, soon after the disaster, she had delivered a speech representing our 9/11 families at a forum with elected state officials at Rutgers University. She hit a home run with her talk and received a standing ovation afterward. Later, I told her, "You just knocked their socks off!" After she had finished her speech, Senator Corzine immediately sprung from his seat off the stage and approached her for her contact information!

JANUARY 31, 2002
THURSDAY: 10:30 a.m.

A puppy named "Honey" made his debut at the group. Pet therapy is always good therapy for all those in grief, especially children. We all melted when we saw little Honey, a Yorkie puppy, pulled out of a small tote bag. His owner, one of our group members, told us the dog had a wardrobe! Honey was the highlight of the day for us! (Honey was named after the group member's husband, who had died on 9/11.)

Michel Baumeister, a noted aviation attorney from Mendham, New Jersey, had called to ask if he could speak to our group about the *Victims Compensation Fund*. I agreed, wanting to give the members all the information they needed to make the right decisions as individuals.

Michel had a relative who lost her husband on 9/11. He told the group that he would not be taking any additional clients, but that he wanted them to be knowledgeable. He discussed the pros and cons of the *Victims Compensation Fund*. Michel had conflicts with the government program, and his clients were women who had decided not to go with the fund. He was hoping that Kenneth Feinberg, Special Master of the U.S. Government's September 11th *Victims Compensation Fund*, would provide more guidance on the next set of regulations. My plan was to get Ken Feinberg on the phone to schedule him to address this group.

February: Valentine's Day & Broken Hearts

"Be on your guard, stand firm in the faith, be courageous, be strong.
Your every act should be done with love."
(1 Cor. 16:13–14)

One of the men in the group called to my attention that our registration was now up to seventy-six families. I never looked at numbers because I was so focused on my work. The registration desk alerted me from time to time on the numbers, but it went over my head. However, I did notice that our room was bursting at the seams. We were going to become a fire hazard, and I was uncomfortable moving into an auditorium to run a support group. We were going to have to come up with some alternatives. The tables of coffee and food had been taken out of the room weeks prior in order for more chairs to take their place. The gathering foyer overflowed. I started channeling new callers to other area groups, with permission from the group leaders. The office of the church received multiple calls from the New York area for entrance into our group. I received one call from a relative who was angry we were channeling people to other groups and wanted only our group. I wondered why there were not more support groups out there. I knew of two in our area and one at the Jersey Shore.

FEBRUARY 7, 2002
THURSDAY: 10:30 a.m.
(76 in attendance)
"WE CELEBRATE YOU, OUR HEROES"

I received a phone call from Ina, a lovely woman from Mountainside, New Jersey. Ina was a member of the Quilt Makers of America, and she offered handmade quilts for all of our children. She then organized quilt makers from all over our country to create the most beautiful quilts to wrap around our now 104 grief-stricken little children, all desperately in need of comfort.

I invited Ina to come and hand out the quilts herself at this meeting. The group needed to see her face of goodness. In turn, she could witness their expressions of wonder and delight when they saw those brightly colored treasures of comfort for the first time. The goodness and compassion of the Quilt Makers of America had been woven into a most special gift of love. The quilts, made to match the gender and age of each child, reflected the utmost care. We will always remember the goodness of these strangers touching our children with their gift of warmth and love.

My eyes were drawn to a striking, and jaw-dropping paper banner with the words "We Celebrate You, Our Heroes" in red, white, and blue adorning the front of the room. Karen, a Basking Ridge resident and the banana bread baker for our group each week, had mentioned that her husband, John Newhouse, who worked for *CNN*, wanted to offer his gift, too, as a graphic artist. John's talent was visible this day on the amazing banner he produced.

Our 9/11 families had worked so hard at their grief work. I really was impressed and inspired by their commitment to heal. It was time to affirm them. Keeping in line with the theme of the day, the group was asked to wear their flag scarves for the meeting. In the auditorium, the volunteers had set up a savory lunch donated to us by Wegmans Food Market in Bridgewater, New Jersey. The Short Hills Hilton Spa in Short Hills, New Jersey, sent us a manicurist. "Healing Touch" therapy set up in rooms down the hall, and a Reiki master came to offer her gift of comfort. We were in full swing all day.

Also present as an observer was Jennifer Barrett, a journalist with *Newsweek®* magazine and a friend of one of the group members. I was hesitant and uncomfortable concerning Jennifer's attendance, but I discussed her proposal to visit with the group. I opted for the group to vote, and they signaled their willingness to let Jennifer observe.

FEBRUARY 14, 2002
THURSDAY: 10:30 a.m.
A VALENTINE'S DAY LIKE NO OTHER!

Today would be a very difficult day. Our 9/11 families would be without their valentines for the first time, and Valentine Days in the past possibly would resurface. It would be a very hard day for them indeed. I had met with the volunteer team two weeks prior to discuss how we would approach the day. Everyone was going to be heavy-hearted, so I wanted our meeting to be light and whimsical. I shared with the volunteers what I had envisioned — a "Valentine Banquet" with silver candelabras, long tables, and brunch.

During our planning, we also discussed what items we could hand out. Many of the families had mentioned plans for a trip with their children to a warmer climate for spring break. One of the volunteers suggested a great idea of a basket full of bottles to be used for "messages in a bottle." They could take the bottles on their vacations or to the Jersey Shore at another time. Kimberly Borin, guidance counselor at the Liberty Corner School, had sent us all kinds of artfully handmade journals, so creatively trimmed in pink and red with satin ribbons. We planned to place a journal at each table setting.

I imagined starting the day with pampering and love all around. I would begin with guided imagery with my old friend Paul Alexander playing a part. Not only is Paul a creative composer and singer, but he is also a resource to aid the bereaved in many ways. Through his CD "Wrap Myself in a Rainbow," Paul would spiritually move the group through a rainbow of colors with guided imagery. I believed it would be a moving, healing, and soothing way to begin the day. Then we would move down the hallway to the arts and crafts room set up by the volunteers. Tables would be supplied with paint pens of many different colors. Everyone would be given a smooth rock and asked to write a word on the rock as a valentine message to their buddy in the group. This "word" might symbolize what each buddy meant to one another. Many might write on their rock the words, Strength, Hope, Healing, I imagined. They could decorate the rocks in different colors with flowers, etc.

Next, we would move back into our room, which was transformed into a Valentine Banquet by our volunteers and food committee. Here we would enjoy a brunch, compliments of a local restaurant. For dessert, donation of a large, heart-shaped cake would be a fitting end to the day. Our meeting concluded.

On a peek through the glass doors of our room on Valentine's Day morning I could view pots of red tulips scattered on tables around the room. Once we were gathered together I began with the guided imagery. We then proceeded down the hall to the arts and crafts project. While we were gone the volunteers and food committee fairies created a Valentine Banquet which was a sight to behold! Long banquet tables were covered in white tablecloths, patterned with pink and red hearts along with matching napkins. Another elegant touch was the gleaming silver candelabras with red, lit candles, compliments of Ken Rent of Bernardsville, New Jersey. Candy kisses and candy hearts inscribed with words of love were scattered down the center of the tables. At each place setting was the journal tied up with pink satin ribbons, along with valentines sent from the Saint James School students. On the serving table were placed platters of delicious food prepared for us by *Tre Vigne'* restaurant in Bernardsville, New Jersey. The brunch was scrumptious and the dessert table was generously adorned with heart shaped sugar cookies, candy kisses and to top it all off was the donation of a large, strawberry and whip cream heart-shaped cake!

For an added touch attendees left with a single red rose, a symbol of the love between them and their lost loved ones. My dreams had all come true for the day, and the volunteers had outdone themselves. Kudos to you, "The Angel Hands Group!" You were surely our Valentines of the day!!

Before we adjourned, I shared with the group that I would be out of the room the following week for a minor same-day simple medical procedure, "nothing serious to worry about," I said. I also finally told them that I was a breast cancer survivor. I was being truthful with them on the recommendation from my doctor and nurse.

As I drove out of the parking lot of the church on this day I was thinking this is a bereavement group like no other!

FEBRUARY 21, 2002
THURSDAY: 10:30 a.m.

The plan for the day was to entwine spirituality and grief through a video created by Dr. James Miller entitled "You Shall Not Be Overcome." Discussion would follow. Since I was out of the meeting for a medical procedure, Staci our social worker and Elise, both facilitators, led the group.

As I arrived home after my outpatient procedure, I found a surprise at my door. Word got around fast in Basking Ridge, I thought! My surprise was the cutest little teddy bear, compliments of a local stitchery group who had called me weeks earlier to inquire about what they might do for the families. I suggested a project, and I could see they were well into action. The group members were thoughtful, and I was deeply touched. (The stitchery ladies would play an extensive role in our group's lives with their gifts of goodness during the upcoming months.)

FEBRUARY 28, 2002
THURSDAY: 10:30 a.m.
"WHEN LIFE GIVE YOU LEMONS, MAKE LEMONADE"

A lot of ideas for our meetings came to me in my dreams. I kept paper and pen next to my bed, so when I dreamed about a thought for a program, I could sit up and jot the idea down. Maybe these notions came to me because this was my quiet time, or perhaps it was God guiding me along the way? Maybe both.

For this particular week, our theme was "When Life Gives You Lemons, Make Lemonade," and I had the idea for John, our graphic artist. While planning the theme, I was a little late contacting John. When I reached him on the phone on Saturday morning, I apologized for calling so late and shared my theme concept. John asked, "Pam, could you dream a little faster?"

John's banner, which hung on the wall, was exceptional as the centerpiece of the theme for the day! His artistry beautifully combined slices of lemons, and lemons and ice cubes in a big glass pitcher of lemonade in 3D. "Way to go, John," I thought. (I marveled at his talent with each new banner he created. *CNN* was lucky to have this man in my opinion.)

From the moment the group entered the building, yellow was dominant. The volunteers had used their fairy-like touches. Real lemons adorned the hospitality tables and were tastefully placed around the room. Large glass vases filled with water, lemons, beautiful daffodils, and yellow tulips dotted the room. Lemon squares, lemon cupcakes, and lemon drops intermingled with whole lemons scattered the tops of the snack tables, which were covered with you guessed it… lemon-colored tablecloths! The team was even asked to wear yellow. I thought we were now becoming the "designer bereavement Group!"

The program planned for the day featured a panel discussion. The panel members shared their stories of loved ones who had died and what the grief process was like. Our facilitator, Fran, shared her experience on the death of a spouse. Virginia, a nurse, and my dear friend, told the story of the death of her parents. Elise talked about the death of her son, Reid. Speaking on the death of a fiancé was Pat, a volunteer, who expressed her feelings on this difficult death. I spoke on the death of my sibling, Joan, and another one of our volunteers spoke on the death of a parent in an Iranian prison. I would also address the issue of compounded loss on this day.

Jennifer Barrett of *Newsweek*® magazine sat in on our meeting again with permission from the group by vote.

Before the official program for the day began, I introduced "The Bear Makin' Ladies," the stitchery group mentioned earlier. I told the story of how this creative and caring group of women in Basking Ridge called me wanting to know how they could reach out to the families of 9/11. About three weeks prior, I first talked to Laurie Summers, one of "The Bear Makin' Ladies," on the phone. She offered to share the group's talent of stitchery, and my antennas instantly went up! I asked if they might have a pattern for teddy bears, and Laurie thought they could drum one up. I proposed my asking the 9/11 families for a shirt belonging to their loved ones who had died. These shirts could be stitched into bears, and the bears could be made for the families to hug.

Just prior to this meeting, I had received another call from Laurie telling me that the project was finished. She invited me to come to her house and see their most delightful little creations. As I entered her home, the most stunning array of multi-colored teddy bears in pink and red, blue, green, yellow, floral, plaid, and stripes set up on Laurie's living room chair and sofa came into view. Over the bears' hearts were Lacoste alligators, Ralph Lauren polo players, Tommy Hilfiger symbols, and soccer and golf insignias — just emblems of all kinds. The bears were attractively decorated with bows around their necks. I was astonished at the creativity they so lovingly expressed in these darling creatures. The women shared with me on my visit that day that, while making the bears, they had decided they should call themselves "The Bear Makin' Ladies." I wholeheartedly agreed! The goodness, compassion, and unconditional love I witnessed from these ladies profoundly moved me that day.

As I was getting ready to leave Laurie's home, one of the ladies began telling me that when I handed out the bears…and then her voice began to quiver. She gathered herself and explained that it was so hard for them to cut into the fabric of the shirts. I told the ladies that I would not be handing out the teddy bears. I wanted the families to see their faces, the faces of goodness! I also asked them to write down their feelings about the making of the bears so their feelings could be shared with our group.

"The Bear Makin' Ladies" arrived at the meeting with arms full of lavishly cellophane-wrapped treasures tied with big puffy white satin bows and streamers of red, white, and blue ribbons flowing from each gift. Not a dry eye was in sight as they handed out the bears and embraced the recipients tightly.

They delivered the following expression of their innermost feelings in creating this project for our group:

I'LL DO ANYTHING BUT CUT

It's not that I was afraid to cut INTO the shirt,
But that I was so afraid of making a mistake
And ruining it,
Ruining the one thing they had given us
To memorialize their loved one's,
The one thing they had chosen
To represent their loss,
The one thing that would give them such unique comfort,
That maybe no other personal belonging could provide.
Where WAS this man?
This man who was supposed to be home with his family tonight.
Eating dinner.
Helping with homework.
Keeping his wife sane.
Here I am
Looking at,

Touching,
Feeling,
Smelling,
This shirt he once wore
On His chest
I can see him in it – faceless.
Golfing.
Working.
Playing.
Laughing.
Loving.
I keep touching it.
Smelling it,
So deeply, that I will never forget,
He will be with me forever,
In this obscure way.
IT is killing me.
I am in disbelief. This was never supposed to happen.
WHY?
Someone please explain to me — WHY?
What shirt would I choose if it were "MY" husband?
The father of "MY" children
What one shirt would capture the essence of his personality?
How could I make such a choice?
Then I saw the short sleeved pink cotton shell.
A shirt I could see any one of us wearing.
The color so female,
The cut so simple and sweet
The loss is so real.
A woman
The nurturer of men and children
How will they manage without her?
No one can replace her
Because no two are the same

Yet somehow — they will survive.
But surviving is a far cry from living.
And that's what we are trying to do.
Helping them to heal so that they may continue.
We are transforming these shirts into priceless,
Timeless items
To be cherished for an eternity.
Teddy Bears that will be loved, hugged, and soaked with tears.
Tears for the lost memories
Tears for the lost years
Tears for the lost time

Written By: Marianne Ryan Pawlicki

Thank you to these wonderfully innovative women for their labor of love! "The Bear Makin' Ladies" team — Laurie Summers, Mary Ellen Peters, Eileen Maxwell, Chris Pape, Michelle Reedy, Kris Koop, Carol Dawson, Brenda Easop, Terry Morano, Nancy Lechleider, Marianne Pawlicki, and last but never least, Joan Dill. Many hearts feel so warm and comforted because of your goodness.

The group made over 140 bears for our group at the time, and some group members ordered more.

REFLECTIONS FROM KRIS KOOP, A BEAR MAKIN' LADY

Being part of "The Bear Makin' Ladies" group has had a profound impact on my life. I don't think any of us could have envisioned the power that this project would have on our lives. At the time I certainly did not.

I just remember feeling grateful. Grateful, that I could help these grieving families. Grateful that maybe my actions and the gift of a little bear could ease the pain and fear that the widows, children, parents and grandparents were experiencing. I was grateful for something tangible to do in a time when fear and sadness gripped our community and nation.

The process of making "our little bears" was a powerful bonding experience for our little group. We cried together when we opened our first bag of shirts and wondered how we could ever cut into these precious articles of clothing. We felt immensely responsible for the clothes and wanted to make something beautiful that would make a difference.

I was blessed to see firsthand the reaction of the widows when we passed out our first batch of bears and knew instantly that we had made a difference. We continued to make our little bears. We received countless thank you notes expressing sincere appreciation, and we learned that our bears provided comfort and love to those grieving their beloved family members who passed on. We have heard many stories of the little bears that have traveled with their owners on vacations, gone to college, and are ever present to people as they have moved on in their lives.

As "The Bear Makin' Ladies" continue to make our little bears for the families, both through the group called "Good Grief" and through word of mouth, I feel proud and blessed to know that our small acts of kindness can make such a difference for so many grieving people. The kind notes and many verbal expressions of gratitude we received made me committed to continuing our bear mission to all those who request a little bear! I know that they are receiving much more than a simple stuffed bear. They are receiving hope and love.

My life has been changed by our bear project. I continue to surround myself with loving and like-minded women who want to give back to others. After going through a personal painful divorce, I know the power of a simple gesture and the comfort and love that wonderful girlfriends provide.

I am a very involved heart-worker and believe in the powerful mission of "Heartworks". I feel blessed to be part of a group of women who want to help others and extend love and hope to those who need it the most. I am privileged to be part of a group that started because of 9/11 and know that so much good has come from this tragic day.

On each anniversary of 9/11, I try to keep the goodness in my thoughts. I don't think about the planes hitting the towers. I think about the light rising up from Ground Zero; the light that continues to shine through little bears and thousands of other random acts of kindness that started that day.

March: Marching Into Spring

Early March

I was not present for the first meeting of the month, and the facilitators carried the ball. The special speakers for the day talked about nutrition and the importance of physical fitness.

On March 11, 2002, the six-month anniversary of 9/11, Jennifer Barrett's article entitled, "The Only Place Where I Feel Safe," released in *Newsweek®*. The group seemed pleased with the article when we discussed it at the following meeting.

MARCH 13, 2002
WEDNESDAY: 1 p.m.
THE SPECIAL MASTER

After our meeting in late January with attorney Michel Baumeister, I called Kenneth Feinberg to invite him to address the group about the *Victims Compensation Fund*. This fund was formed by an act of Congress after 9/11 to compensate the surviving families in exchange to agree not to sue airlines involved. Known as the "Special Master," Mr. Feinberg was appointed by Attorney General John Ashcroft. I was impressed by the fact learned during my preliminary research that his work was performed on a pro-bono basis and learning later his work was over a thirty – three – month period. We scheduled a special meeting in addition to our regular weekly meeting in order to accommodate Mr. Feinberg's schedule and allow for enough time for discussion.

Today it was a full house when the so-called "Special Master" entered the room. His articulate delivery on the *Victims Compensation Fund* was clear and informative, and he seemed comfortable with the group. Lots of questions were asked, and he had answers for everyone.

I observed that there was a mutual respect for the man, and I noted a compassionate tone for those he was addressing, some even by name.

MARCH 14, 2002
THURSDAY: 10:30 a.m.
THE QUILT MAKER

At today's meeting, we observed the six-month anniversary of 9/11. After opening the day with prayer, we took a guided imagery trip to Ireland for St. Patrick's Day, since it was to be celebrated in just three more days. Oh, it was a grand time that we spent in the midst of Irish imagery and the green fields!

During our candle-lighting ritual, rocking, swaying, and humming were all pointed out as good and positive coping mechanisms.

Sarah Roberts, a quilt maker, came and showed different quilts she had resourcefully created. Some of the girls discussed making a quilt with their husbands' clothes. One of our girls cleverly designed a quilt made out of her husband's clothes that she planned to give to her daughter. It was a spectacular project and a great example of transformative grief. I just loved the creativity!

On this six-month anniversary, I observed that the group was now beginning to eat. Progress… their appetites were coming back!

Today we welcomed two speakers, a financial consultant from Paine Webber and Annie Greenleaf, whose name I had received from the YMCA in Basking Ridge.

Annie opened her presentation about Journaling with the following prayer:

My Dear Children,

Do you think that your heavy-weighted hearts go unnoticed? Could I send you my beloved children into this world where strife may strike at any moment and leave a wound so deep, that one may think the end has come? No not I, dear one, for I am the Father of unconditional love. It is I who gave you life. It is I who understands your every feeling, deed, thought, and emotion. You are in my firm hand and I am holding you always. When you think there is an angel around you, know that there are thousands.

If you are looking for the Master, do not look ahead for He is right by your side.

And when you lift your head up to the heavens and call on Me, My firm grip of love is holding you tighter than ever.

Annie Greenleaf

Annie discussed journaling and gave us new and in depth perspectives on the topic. The time with Annie proved to be most beneficial indeed, and we thoroughly enjoyed the information she shared.

I am an advocate of letter writing to the deceased and to God, as part of journaling. That is especially so in this situation, as there was no time to say goodbye to their beloved person. Letter writing is a powerful way to share feelings with their loved one. It can also be helpful to write a letter from that person back to you. You knew them well, so what would they have said to you? At times I assigned homework for our members to write a letter to their loved one and draft a letter from them back. I also asked them to write to God and have Him write back to you what would he say, as your loving Father, in reply? I encouraged those who wrote letters to burn the letters in their backyards and let the smoke rise to the heavens. I have used this exercise with grievers many times in the past.

Filling our room on this day was an abundant golden display of spring's delight. One of the women in our group donated daffodils for all of us. The daffodils were from a golf tournament given to memorialize her husband, who was a victim of 9/11. I recognized this golf tournament as transformative grief in action, sprouting up into the garden of new life. Yes, it was surely a glimpse of springtime.

After the meeting, Julie Lee and Pat McNamee planted the remaining daffodils around the "Tree of Memory" we had planted in late November outside the church doors.

MARCH 28, 2002
THURSDAY: 10:30 a.m.
HOLY THURSDAY "DO THIS IN REMEMBRANCE OF ME"

As we sat around the room, we reflected on what the high-holy day of Holy Thursday meant for Christians. I then read the scripture:

> "For I received from the Lord what I also handed down on to you, that the Lord Jesus on the night he was handed over, took bread, and, after he had given thanks, broke it and said, "This is my body that is for you. Do this in remembrance of me." In the same way also the cup, after supper, saying, "This cup is the new covenant in my blood. Do this, as often as you drink

it, in remembrance of me." For as often as you eat this bread and drink this cup, you proclaim the death of the Lord until He comes."
(1 Cor. 11:23–26)

I thought about the beautiful souls who died on 9/11. Just as Jesus was to give up His life, so too, did they give up their lives. Jesus realized what was to happen to Him, but these 9/11 victims never knew what was going to happen to them on such a disastrous gruesome day.

As a group, we explored together the actions that they and their families could take to keep their deceased loved ones' names alive and what they could do in remembrance of them.

After lunch, one of our participants gave a presentation about the ritual of Passover, also being celebrated on this day. We had several Jewish individuals in our group, and I wanted to address their faith, too. It is through education that I believe we can better appreciate the faiths of our fellow brothers and sisters.

Grape juice and unleavened bread were passed around. We ended the day with prayer and an Agape of love.

WE REMEMBER THEM

In the rising of the sun
And in its going down,
We remember them.

In the blowing of the wind
And in the chill of winter,
We remember them.

In the opening of buds
And in the warmth of summer,
We remember them.

In the beginning of the year
And when it ends,
We remember them.

When we are weary
And in need of strength,
We remember them.

When we are lost
And sick of heart,
We remember them.

When we have joys
We yearn to share,
We remember them.

So long as we live they too shall live,
For they are now a part of us,
As we remember them.

"Gate of Repentance" The New Union Prayer Book of Awe
A litany of Remembrance by Rabbi Sylvan
Kamens and Rabbi Jack Reimer

**On this day we also handed out voting forms for a chairperson and co-chairperson. These individuals would continue to unite the group after our weekly meetings concluded.

REFLECTIONS FROM PAT McNAMEE, FACILITATOR

I garnered more from the surviving spouses, parents, siblings, and children then I gave. In the group, I witnessed such authentic raw emotion and compassion. The very vulnerability of 9/11 families made them beautiful. Their determination to breathe and go on was utterly inspirational. I was awed by the group's great faith in spite of suffering the loss of their dearest loved ones, especially in such a horrific manner. I believe that not only their faith, but also their courage and compassion led me to deepen and strengthen my own faith and trust in God. It spurred me to an even deeper love and commitment to my family and friends.

April: Guided Imagery and Journaling

pril started off with two special meetings. First, Lin, a financial advisor with Wachovia Securities, visited and answered many questions for the families.

Then, in place of our regular meeting on April 4, some of our members attended a "Creative Memories" scrapbooking session at the Basking Ridge home of a local woman named Pam Dorodo. She wanted to share her gift of scrapbooking with those who were available to attend. (Many were away for the Easter holiday and spring break, myself included.) The members who attended stated the session was inspiring and innovative. One of the girls made beautiful memory books that she later shared with me. Her treasures were a delight to marvel at and a creation to cherish.

Pam's gift and outreach to our group sparked a new hobby through which several of the 9/11 families kept memories alive. How much better this world would be if we could just accept each other, live kindly, and share our gifts with others, as Pam did on this day.

She was just one of the many people of goodness. Sometimes I think that the goodness coming our way was like looking through a kaleidoscope up into the sun. We see so many angles and different shades and shapes of colors. An illustrious sight to behold! People with all kinds of talents were sharing their goodness and love with us. It was their vibrant light, like the light in the kaleidoscope pointed and shining upon us for all to see.

APRIL 11
THURSDAY: 10:30 a.m.
SPECIAL GUESTS

Before the meeting started, we introduced two guests related to Julie Lee, one of our volunteers. Julie's sister Nancy and her fifth-grade daughter, Molly, from Arlington Heights, Illinois, were visiting with Julie for Easter vacation. They told us that Molly's school, Our Lady of the Wayside, held a t-shirt sale to benefit the families of 9/11. They sold red shirts with "Wayside Cares" written on them and the towers placed in a big heart. How nice to welcome these beautiful people from Illinois, and we admired them for their goodness in every way.

Elise began the group meeting by reading "The Butterfly Poem." Butterfly balloons graced the room, and on each seat rested an egg, the symbol of new life during the season of spring. Inside every egg were a penny and a small chocolate egg. I pointed out the messages conveyed by the items — "In God We Trust" and the "sweetness" in the chocolate egg. I asked the group to give the eggs to people in their loved ones' names. I pointed out that this was symbolizing a transformative grief reaction.

We welcomed back our fiancés' group who would visit from time to time, including today, to hear our special guest, my friend Heidi Snow. Heidi brought her chocolate egg to us in her inspiring story of transformative grief reaction. She was a heartening and dynamic speaker. Heidi's fiancé, Michel Breistroff, died when *TWA Flight 800* exploded and crashed into the Atlantic Ocean after take off on July 17, 1996. All 230 people on board perished. Heidi grieved deeply after the loss, but emerged from her pain to create the Aircraft Casualty Emotional Support Services (ACCESS). What a privilege it was to have her with us and how encouraging, also, to hear her words of wisdom. To this day, Heidi is a catalyst of healing for so many and has surely made a difference. She has brought Michel's goodness back into the world through aiding others.

APRIL 18, 2002
THURSDAY: 10:30 a.m.
JOURNALING DREAMS

For our twenty-seventh session, I decided to take the group to new surroundings and out into the light. It was springtime in the Northeast, and the weather was getting warmer. Basking Ridge has exceptional recreational facilities, and I chose Harry Dunham Park for this meeting. We met in a glass room overlooking the park-like setting. The sun glistened through the large, full-length, picture windows onto all the faces present in the room. It was the perfect place!

I invited Annie Greenleaf back due to popular demand and asked her to speak on "Journaling Dreams." When you see someone who has died in your dream, the dream is called a "visitation dream." This kind of dream is usually very real and vivid, and you awake from it in a peaceful state. There can be communication with the person who looks well, not sickly, and who lets you know that he or she is okay. Annie talked to us about how to record the dreams and the impact they had on us. I share with you I did experience a "visitation dream" when I lost my mother.

I suggested the group get out and exercise since the park was the perfect place for it. The walking trails were just delightful, a place I myself frequented. I reminded and encouraged the group once again to listen to soft music as they walked along or to bring their buddy with them. I reminded them that increased exercise would help them to sleep better. I constantly reminded them about different aspects of grief and the tools to help them because the bereaved, sometimes being overwhelmed, needed to be reminded. They can be forgetful at times, which is common to people immersed in grief and the bereavement process.

APRIL 25, 2001
THURSDAY: 10:30 a.m.
IN THE GARDEN by Susun Weed /"BRIGHTEST COLOR DAY"

Today I was dressed in my garden clothes, complete with a straw hat and apron. I opened the meeting with *In the Garden*, written by Susun Weed. Guided imagery is a beneficial tool to ameliorate the painful feelings during bereavement, and it also leads to relaxation. I began the exercise with lights dimmed and candles lit. I asked all to take off their shoes if they would like to, get into a comfortable position I directed, and close your eyes, consciously taking in a deep breath through the nose, releasing the breath slowly through the mouth. We continued breathing like this a couple of more times and then proceeded with even breathing.

I guided the group through to the garden. Today we will plant a garden. Together we will decide what we will plant in that garden and how we might protect it from harm. I located them in the garden through imagery, describing them like saplings sprouting through the dirt, green in hope and promise, yet still fragile with dirt on their sides. We planted peas: peace of heart and peace of soul. We planted lettuce: lettuce be kind, lettuce be thankful, and lettuce really love one another. We planted thyme: thyme for family and thyme for each other. We planted several other plantings that Susun Weed so creatively put on paper in her poem. We planted the seeds under the sun and built a fence to keep the garden safe from predators. We had water available to nurture the garden and help it grow. I encouraged the group members to envision themselves sharing the harvest with others, and then I invited them walking back into the room.

I told the group at the previous meeting, that we would be having a contest called the "Brightest Color Day" at our next meeting. Spring had sprung, leaving behind a dreary winter indeed. Bringing color into the room was my hope to stimulate the senses. The person dressed in the brightest colors would receive a prize. One girl, Jeanne, was the winner, hands down. She went home with a prize donated to us from Tommy Hilfiger.

May: Signs of Hope

MAY 2, 2002
THURSDAY: 10:30 a.m.
CAMP COMFORT/CLINICAL CHILDHOOD PSYCHOLOGY

Today marked the second visit from volunteers, Pat Lunny and Marion G., both members of St. Mark Episcopal Church in Basking Ridge. They introduced Lynn Hughes, a representative from Camp Comfort. Lynn gave a presentation about the children's camp, and many of the group's children later attended camp and found it most beneficial.

An observation: Families who participated in camp returned to our group and shared that they themselves were further along in the grief process than other 9/11 families they met at camp who were not part of our group.

The second part of the day featured a presentation by Dr. Beatrice Beebe, PhD, a clinical professor of Medical Psychology (in Psychiatry) at Columbia University and New York State Psychiatric Institute. Their research focused on infants and small children of September 11, 2001. Several of our group signed up and traveled into New York City to participate in a therapy project co-directed by Dr. Phyllis Cohen.

MAY 9, 2002
THURSDAY: 10:30 a.m.
OPENING: A PRAYER FOR MOTHERS

We were inching toward Mother's Day. I asked the group how they were feeling, and we explored how to go forward. At eight months since the deaths, all in the group had accepted the reality of the loss. Sometimes guilt over moving forward might surface, I told them. In past groups, I have heard grievers mention how, for one hour during the day, they forgot about their lost loved one. Then they described how they felt guilty as a result. I pointed out to the 9/11 families that we could look at this in another way too — this could also be a sign of the beginning of healing.

I handed out a blue sheet of paper featuring a picture of a tree limb sloping upwards with children climbing on it. Some children were high up in the tree, some were hanging on for dear life, and some had fallen to the ground. I asked the group where they thought they might be on the tree of grief, as I called it. While their answers indicated for me where they might be, I told them they could be in another spot at any given time. Since grief comes in waves, they could be anywhere, but to see oneself climbing upward, more times than not, was a sign of progress. Everyone could be in a different place, and it was okay to be in that different spot. You are just where you are. There is no right place and no wrong place; there is only your place. Some people might want to hold onto their grief, I mentioned, and that was just where that person was at, and it was okay. I explained how the grief would come and go and would always be a part of their lives. It would resurface at unexpected times and especially during special occasions, such as graduations, weddings, birthdays, holidays, and anniversaries, or when hearing songs, seeing foods, or visiting places, and even unexpectedly twenty years later. It would be normal to feel the feelings at these times. All of that residual grief was now a part of them.

We discussed the early, razor-sharp edges of the grief from when they first came to the group and initially reacted to the separation.

We recollected and re-examined what had occurred as a result of the loss. I suspected that exploring and softening the edges of their grief through their interaction, communication, and meeting with people who did survive, might have strengthened them. The group had a constant dedication to their grief work at this point.

Once again, we discussed the tools to help them through the difficult times. I asked them, "who wished to go forward," and every hand went up. I then read an exercise about feelings of going forward. We had received hand held mirrors from a hair salon each person looked into the mirror and repeated after me the feelings of going forward and not being alone.

The grief evident in the room was a traumatic complicated grief. The feelings of pain and grief would linger on. I realized it was still early and a long way off that the group needed more time to relinquish old attachments, adopt new ways of being in the world. I had noticed some changes.

MAY 16, 2002
THURSDAY: 7:00 p.m.
THE CONCERT OF HOPE

The night had come for Paul Alexander's Concert of Hope. I had met Paul at a conference at the National Catholic Ministry to The Bereaved in Belleville, Illinois, and then again at another conference at the New England Center for Loss and Transition in Stamford, Connecticut. Paul's company is called "Griefsong" (griefsong.com) and by now, his music was well known to our group. I had played his music for the candle-lighting ritual, prayer services, the blessing of the Christmas tree, and the balloon launch. I invited Paul to perform this evening so the group could finally meet him in person.

Paul wrote and sang a new song for 9/11 families entitled "Song for America." Paul's music was spiritual and emotive, his voice soothing. His expertise touched the heart of the matter. It was a very moving night for all of us and food for the broken hearts and hurting souls.

Monsignor Capik came to the concert and was impressed by the experience.

I tried to get Paul into the Ground Zero memorials, but to no avail. Paul was the golden thread who led us by music into ways of healing, and he was most supportive of our group. We will always be filled with gratitude to him. Paul Alexander, LSCW-R, a psychotherapist, singer, songwriter, author, and performing artist, not only gives concerts, but also retreats, and workshops, too; Paul's work is inspirational as he focuses on integrating "Energy with Healing."

MAY 21, 2002
TUESDAY: 10:30 a.m.
A KIND INVITATION

We had a kind invitation extended to us by Marion F., the coordinator of the Rumson 9/11 families group in Monmouth County, New Jersey. Marion invited our group to join their group and attend, "Welcome to a Day for Yourself," held at Stella Maris Retreat Center on the water at the Jersey Shore. This delightful day focused on body, mind, and spirit and was filled with alternative therapy, workshops, and lunch. After a beautiful mass with liturgical dance, we proceeded to the rear of the building overlooking the water where we released butterflies into the air. Just a glorious day for all of us!

MAY 23, 2002
THURSDAY: 10:30 a.m.
A DAY OF AEROBICS AT THE SOMERSET HILLS YMCA

We took a break from our regular meeting and headed to the YMCA for an aerobics workout. It was truly uplifting and energizing for all of us.

The Somerset Hills YMCA, under the directorship of Bob Lamauro, was most corroborative with our group. Soon after our group formed, Bob arranged for me to meet with Allen Reese who was the United

Way's president in Somerset County, and Sister Elizabeth O'Hara, a Catholic Charities case manager for family financial stabilization in Somerset County. Bob, Allen, and Sr. Elizabeth worked very hard to aid the 9/11 families in our area. Together, they coordinated outreach to the families.

MAY 30, 2002
THURSDAY
A CHOICE DAY

Today was a "Choice Day" where group members could choose between two events: the closing ceremony at Ground Zero or a visit to a group member's house at the Jersey Shore. (I was not present at either function.)

Some of the group members attended the closing ceremony at Ground Zero, which signified the end of the cleanup and recovery efforts. Personally, I watched the ceremony on the evening news, and it seemed to be a well thought out and solemn event. An honor guard made up of NYPD, FDNY, and first responders stood along the sides of the construction ramp leading out of the Ground Zero disaster area. Police and firemen carried a lone, empty stretcher, symbolizing all those who were not recovered in the days following 9/11. Next appeared an FDNY ambulance, which slowly advanced up the ramp away from the site. Moving out of the area and up the ramp behind the ambulance was a large tractor-trailer hauling the last piece of steel covered in a black shroud and an American flag. A group of NYPD, FDNY, and PAPD bagpipers marched together. At one point, the familiar faces of Governor George Pataki of the State of New York, the former Mayor, Rudy Giuliani of New York City, and the newly elected Mayor, Michael Bloomberg came into view. The entire cortège was executed richly in symbolism. This ritual completed the recovery effort at Ground Zero, and now the rebuild could begin. This day marked eight months and nineteen days since the disaster.

June: Golden Memories

Our group was invited to a luncheon and a fashion show given by the Junior Fortnightly Club in Summit, New Jersey. This event was lovingly, arranged by two club members. Nancy Leccese (my sweet sister-in-law) and her sidekick, Kelly Sandulli did a fabulous job! It was a delightful day for those who attended. Our spirits were lifted by the warmth and generosity of Nancy, Kelly, and all the club members. Thank you to the hearts of gold!

JUNE 6, 2002
THURSDAY: 10:30
"GOLDEN MEMORY DAYS"

Today was a theme day! I thought this day was in order, and an action-packed day it would be. Many members of our group had birthdays, as well as wedding anniversaries, coming around at this time. I knew this would be a trying time for them since they would experience these occasions without their loved ones. I wanted to find a special way to honor their loved ones. This was also a filming day for a segment that *60 Minutes* was producing for the first anniversary. As part of that segment, the show's crew was doing a story on one of our group members. (The group had voted to allow the crew to attend our meeting.)

A few weeks earlier, I called my friend Sally Tracy of Chatham, New Jersey who was well known for her business in baking scrumptious cakes and cookies. I told her my thought about a program with a theme of "Golden Memory Day's." Sally told me she had been wishing she could do something as a gift for the families of 9/11 and thanked me for giving her the opportunity to make a cake. Little did we know what Sally was cooking up!

Yes, graphic artist John Newhouse was at it once again, gracing us with one of his momentous banners. Upon entering the room, our eyes focused on the beautiful banner, featuring a large golden balloon emblematic of the sun and the words "Golden Memory Day's." On both sides of the banner, a bevy of yellow and white balloons floated in mid-air.

We started with a candle-lighting prayer service followed by storytelling and reminiscing for the first part of the day. Our focus was **Residual Grief**. We said a prayer of thanksgiving for all the gifts that their loved ones had given to them.

I had asked the group members to bring in framed wedding pictures, birthday celebration pictures, or any other memorable images of their deceased ones'. Now seen for the first time the faces of those loved ones' in a happier time of life behind a glass and leather frame.

I had also asked the group to bring their loved ones' favorite foods. What an array of delicacies we had! Meatballs and watermelons and many more savory delights covered the tables. It was a phenomenal day as they shared their stories and reminisced how they would always remember their loved ones relishing the food brought in that day. Honestly, everyone laughed and cried during this time.

I always like to sprinkle a bit of humor into a group where I see fit. Humor plays an important role in the grief process, taking the edge off at times. (I would say it is a positive coping mechanism.) During lunch, I could not help but remark on the plate of yodels piled high with powdered sugar all over them. What a creation this member accomplished with yodels!

I then explained **Residual Grief**. "Two years from now or ten years from now, when you open that refrigerator and see the watermelon on the shelf that he or she just loved, the tears might spring forth. This is what we call **Residual Grief**. It could also be that your loved one's favorite song will come on the radio in your car, causing the tears to flow. It is okay, it is just how it is, and it is normal even if it is years later. This emotional response is because you loved."

As lunch wound down, Sally, my cake-making friend, walked in carrying an enormous box. She unveiled a five-tiered wedding cake, decorated spectacularly with many small American flags adorning the top. What a sight to behold! We were all amazed!

For the third and final portion of the day, I had invited two speakers: the trial lawyer, Chris Placitella and Steven Push from the *National Organization of Families for September 11*. Chris was most accomplished in his field in New Jersey, and he spoke on the *Victims Compensation Fund*, ending his time engaging in discussion and answering questions. Stephen came from Great Falls, Virginia, and had left his job when his wife Lisa died in the Pentagon on 9/11. He became the co-founder of *National Organization of Families for September 11*. He talked about his efforts to aid the families and push the government to strengthen the fight against terrorism. He, too, gave a presentation that was most informative. Questions followed from the group.

After nearly five hours, we closed our meeting in prayer.

JUNE 13, 2002
THURSDAY: 10:30
"SAILING TOWARD HOPE"

Theme Day once again! We started with a presentation to Monsignor Capik for Father's Day. Monsignor was such an outstanding individual who had given his life to God's people. He was devoted to the victims and their families. I had purchased a replica of a sailboat and, at a prior meeting, asked for a volunteer in the group to paint on it USS *WTC 9/11 SURVIVOR SHIP*. Someone immediately raised a hand. Then I asked for a volunteer to write a dedication letter to Monsignor, and immediately more hands went up. The letter was read to him on this day of tribute as follows:

HAPPY FATHER'S DAY, MONSIGNOR CAPIK

In the journey of life, difficult times and obstacles appear when we least expect them. Circumstances change; plans and dreams fail; people that we care about may be taken away from us. Suddenly the road we have been traveling with such confidence and hope turns in a direction we never anticipated or it even disappears. On September 11, 2001, our community, our world, for that matter, was drowning in a sea of contemplated death, destruction, and evil of unknown proportions. The terrorist attacks in our country momentarily made us question life, liberty, freedom, and safety. Many people questioned their faith in God.

Reminiscent of the way Jesus saved His apostles from the storm on the lake, Monsignor Capik saved so many of us. It was then that Jesus, acting through this disciple on earth, created our bereavement group. He gathered other disciples and inspired people of many faiths to reach out to those of us who lost our loved ones. He struggled with us to find the meaning behind these events and the way beyond them. With compassion and candor, Monsignor provided a source of comfort, reassurance, and enlightenment to encourage us on our journey. He showed us that with God we are not alone; He is with us every step of the way. We all must persevere through the challenges of life and share our gifts with others. We thank you, Monsignor Capik, for sharing yourself with us. You are a voice of hope and inspiration.

We present you with this ship as a symbol that kept us afloat and the safe place to harbor us here at Saint James. Thank you, dear Monsignor, your goodness and kindness will always be remembered.

We thank God for your vocation to His Priesthood and the wisdom you had to shelter us in the storm. You have truly been a father to us and we wish you a very Happy Father's Day.

Katy Soulas

After many hugs, Monsignor left the room. I swiftly directed the group into breathing exercises. Lights set low, I asked them to position themselves in a comfortable way and invited them to close their eyes to begin the breathing techniques. I then flowed into guided imagery, placing them in the following scenario entitled "A Day Just For Me"!

"I now step off a dock into a highly polished white and navy-blue sloop, an American flag waving in the warm winds at the stern of the boat. The sun is shining brightly above me, and I apply my Bobbi Brown sunscreen. It is a day just for me... me to be free from all worries, and I gently float off into the cool aquamarine waters below. The crisp white sails filling fully with the winds are moving the boat in a westerly direction. In the sky, seagulls coo in the soft breeze. Alongside me, a school of dolphins is splashing and dancing in the waves of the boat, and a rainbow rises far off in the distance... I continued the guided imagery further, we then finish our voyage rocking gently and serenely floating into the wooden dock at The Port of Saint James." We completed our exercise then walking back into our room.

I had started this group with the scripture from Matthew 8:23 depicting Jesus in the boat with His friends in the storm. My thought for using the guided imagery was the group coming out of the storm floating in a new direction toward hope with the sun shinning brightly above.

Quite a few other notable events happened on this day. We had an appearance of "The Bear Makin' Ladies," bringing more teddy bears for the families. The ladies shared with us that they had become so inspired by our group they were going to begin training for a bike ride from Ground Zero to Washington, DC, for the first anniversary, thus becoming "The Bear Makin' Bikin' Ladies." What an amazing story!

The filming crew from *60 Minutes* returned to continue filming a member of the group as part of a segment on the first anniversary of 9/11. They wanted to show her attending our group.

On the chairs in the room was Josh Groban's latest CD. I had contacted his company and asked for a donation for the Father's Day meeting. I also mentioned that we used his music for many of our programs. His generous gift was received three days later. His songs were soothing and many related to the bereaved group members. "You Raise Me Up" and "Your Still You," are both songs I have used many times. I must mention, here, Paul Alexander's song, "Who Am I Now" – This is also a song that addresses identity. "Am I still a mother? Am I still a Mrs.? Who am I now without you? Who am I supposed to be?" It is not uncommon to question your identity when a loved one has died. I remember a mother of one of the girls in the group asking me if her daughter would ever be the same again. I replied, "it was my hope after the group was over she would be stronger than ever before." It was my hope that she would do great things. As time has past she is stronger than before and has taken amazing actions in her husband's name. Her choice was to go to a higher plateau and she has done just that.

Weeks earlier, I had written renowned makeup artist and New Jersey resident Bobbi Brown and asked her to come and do a presentation on makeup. My idea was taken from "Look Good Feel Better," a program for those battling cancer. On this day, the weather was warm, the feeling was right, and Bobbi was a delight to work with. From the group, she selected three women to make up, one mom who had lost her son and two women who had lost husbands. We had an incredible day and thanked Bobbi for sharing her goodness and many gifts with us. She sparkled and elevated our spirits at such a difficult time.

With Father's Day approaching on the next weekend, it was going to be a difficult time. The question in all our minds was, "how is this day going to be?" I handed out prayers to be shared around the table at dinner for Father's Day. The families also received candles to light and place in front of a photo of their loved one for the day. We read the prayer together to end another full day.

Observation: At the closure of the meeting, the group seemed to be on a positive level. At the same time, I knew many were probably experiencing anticipatory grief as they moved closer to Father's Day without their loved one. A sad day it would be, indeed.

REFLECTIONS FROM MONSIGNOR WILLIAM CAPIK

When I look back on 9/11, I think how swiftly I went right to work. Eleven families in the Church of Saint James in Basking Ridge, New Jersey, where I was the pastor, had lost loved ones. In total, in our town, eighteen innocent people had lost their lives in this tragic event. Families were in deep grief. I made daily visits to their homes to be present to them. I aided the families in planning the Memorial Masses. What came to my mind during those early days after the event of 9/11 was the scripture below:

THE BEATITUDES
"Blessed are the poor in spirit, for theirs is the Kingdom of Heaven"
"Blessed are those who mourn, for they will be comforted."
(Matt. 5:3-4)

It was a time of the evident feeling as well as the witness of Divine Intervention. It was truly a God moment of generosity. The unconditional love of the people motivated all of us. The will of God was ever present. For two years, God's presence and power were always with us to share His love, comfort, compassion, and healing to those who grieved. We attempted to assist God the best ways we could with His mission.

Celebrating Our Volunteers

*The Fruit of silence is
Prayer
The Fruit of prayer is
Faith
The Fruit of Faith is
Love
The Fruit of love is
Service.
The Fruit of Service is
Peace.
Saint Teresa of Calcutta*

EARLY JUNE 2002

P rior to the last meeting, I had received a call from Pat Hughes, who was the assistant to Father Peter Krebs, the director of the nearby Shrine of Saint Joseph. She invited me to attend a meeting to plan for the dedication of a bell tower, a local memorial that was being created from the steel of the World Trade Center. The memorial would be located in Stirling, New Jersey, about a mile and a half from the room our group had occupied for the last nine months at Saint James Church. I was sure this was not a coincidence that God saw fit to make this happen in our own backyard! Grateful that we had one more place to perform ritual, I eagerly accepted the invitation to join Father Peter and his team for the meeting.

Upon entering the meeting room, I was warmly greeted by Father Peter and Pat Hughes. They directed me to a seat next to Mr. Raymond Donovan, who was introduced as the benefactor and leader of the project. Father Peter continued the introductions to the other team members. The job they wanted to assign me was to send invitations for the dedication to the 9/11 families. Eager to help out, I gladly agreed, and Pat handed me a stack of invitations.

I was also asked if I might be able to select someone from our group to give a presentation. That was easy enough, as we already had our spokeswoman. (I hoped she would be available!) Following the meeting, I was given a tour of the phenomenal site. I left and got right to work addressing the invitations and then passing them out at our next meeting with encouragement to attend. I was hoping that the dedication would be a success.

A few days later, an idea came to me. Nine months had passed since we formed the group, and I felt it was time for the families to give back in a small way. For one, we needed to celebrate our volunteers, who had been so steadfast in their support. I called the Shrine's office to see if our group might be able to schedule a picnic for our volunteers and a "Prayer Service of Thanksgiving" on the grounds of the Shrine before the day of the dedication. My wish was granted! Invitations to our "Thank You Picnic" were sent to all the volunteers, as well as Mr. Donovan and his family.

JUNE 20, 2002
THURSDAY: 11:00 a.m.

SAINT JAMES 9/11
BEREAVEMENT SUPPORT GROUP
INVITES "YOU,"
OUR VOLUNTEERS
TO A "THANK YOU PICNIC"

DATE: THURSDAY, JUNE 20
PLACE: SAINT JOSEPH SHRINE
STIRLING, NEW JERSEY
TIME: 11:00 A.M.
GIVEN: WITH LOVE BY THE FAMILIES OF 9/11

***At 12 O'CLOCK THE BELLS WILL RING
FOR US!

Now it was a day for our volunteers who served us well. We would gather together around the newly constructed bell tower and enjoy a picnic lunch!

We made up big buttons that we would pin on the volunteers. The buttons read, **St. James 9/11 Support Group / God Bless America's Volunteers.** We met at the tower at 11 a.m. as construction workers were putting the final touches on the area. We stood arm-in-arm for a "Prayer Service of Thanksgiving" for our volunteers. We could never be more grateful to these beautiful human beings who had given so much of their time and energy, unconditionally, to promote healing, they were the peacemakers and their love and out reach of service was commendable.

THE ORDER OF SERVICE

WELCOMING: Pam Koch

I welcomed the group and thanked Father Peter Krebs and the Shrine for hosting us on this special and meaningful day at the illustrious bell tower. I continued by saying, "This is a sacred place in which to pray and reflect. It is holy ground where we will come to remember. Saint Joseph is the patron Saint of Workers. This is a most fitting place, indeed, to erect this bell tower. We come here this day of July 20, 2002, to remember our workers, our loved ones who lost their precious lives on September 11, 2001, as they went to their workplaces on that horrific day. We applaud the workers who constructed this bell tower and the ingenious idea and generous gift of Mr. Raymond Donovan, whose insight made this amazing creation happen. We celebrate today with thanksgiving in our hearts for other workers, too. It was you, the many workers, who came to our aid and embraced our families affected by the tragedy of September 11, 2001. Volunteer workers reached out from the community of Saint James Church and other churches in our town. People from the areas surrounding Basking Ridge and from all over our country touched us with kindness. God has shed His grace on us and has crowned His good with brotherhood and sisterhood through the blessed hands of our volunteers, and for that, we are most grateful."

A Thanksgiving message from the 9/11 families followed:

A LETTER OF APPRECIATION FROM THE FAMILIES OF 9/11

> *Nine Months. Seems like nine years, at times nine days. That day, the whole world changed, irrevocably for each of us. We were suddenly plunged into an unrelenting darkness, a place where most of us had never before visited. And then out of the gloom came a bright light in the form of a bevy of angels. Angels who reached to pull*

us back from the abyss, to provide us with a safe harbor in which to land.

I will never forget those first few meetings at Saint James. I recall looking around the room at the scared faces of so many strangers who looked just like I did — faces with haunted eyes, rimmed red from too many tears; hearts so broken you could almost hear them weeping, not knowing who to turn to, who to trust.

Somehow, we were guided there to that room where explanations are not necessary.

Where you cannot say anything wrong. Where there is always a shoulder or thirty to cry on. Where candles glow softly and the coos of newborn miracles can be heard, a place, where we feel secure, protected, and loved.

So much has happened on this continuing journey. We have weathered storms that would send the most seasoned sailor scrambling for cover. We have been pushed beyond the limits of what human beings should ever have to endure.

Yet the vacant, scared eyes now show signs of optimism and light. There are still many tears, but there is also laughter and hope.

The reasons for this significant transformation are with us today. You need only to look around you at the faces of these angels that were sent to us to save us from drowning.

Pam, you and these amazing facilitators and volunteers have overwhelmed us with your generosity and selflessness. You put such incredible thought and creativity into making Thursday mornings so special for us. From the beautiful matching plates and napkins to the candles and hand towels in the bathroom. Thank you for taking precious time away from your families to reach out to ours. Thank you for caring for our children when you *have many of your own. Thank you for coming so early in the morning to set up the beautiful tables of food and for sticking around afterward to clean up. Thank you for calling people on our behalf to offer us books, scarves, and teddy bears, among other things, and for sharing with us your own stories of pain and grief that let us know we will be okay. I think I speak for all of us when I say we will never forget you and all you have done for us.*

May God bless all of you and your families and the entire Saint James 9/11 Bereavement Support Group Volunteers!

Laura Maler

A BLESSING OF THE TOWER:

I asked the families of 9/11 to come forward and place their hands on the bell tower. I then made it a joint effort, asking the volunteers, the construction workers present, as well as the Donovan family, to follow suit. I asked them to repeat after me. "Bless this bell tower, oh God may it be a lasting symbol of remembrance of the victims of 9/11 it was erected for. May the bells of this tower of strength echo loudly their names and the love we have for them in our hearts. O Lord, hear our prayer, Amen."

POEM:

One of the 9/11 family members then read, *We Remember Them,* a Litany of Remembrance from The New Union Prayer Book of Awe.

LITANY OF NAMES:

As we read the Litany of Names, I invited those present to toll the bell in their loved one's name, using the mallet on the table before the tower.

CLOSING:

Guest singer Pat Giammarinaro closed the ceremony with her lovely rendition of "God Bless America."

After the service we transitioned to a picnic lunch served on festive red and white checked tablecloths and decorated with red, white, and blue balloons. The serving tables were graced by an array of delicious-looking salads brought by every 9/11 participant in our group. At the center of them all was a large cake reading, "God Bless Our Volunteers." We ended the day hugging in the light of camaraderie with all our hearts filled with love!

Observation: At nine months since the deaths, many of the families radiated glimpses of peace for the first time. I saw numerous faces with smiles on this day.

REFLECTIONS FROM DOLORES CIRRA, VOLUNTEER

Many of those affected, including myself, felt a very strong need to mobilize and help one another. When I found out about The Saint James 9/11 Bereavement Support Group, I joined immediately because I wanted to help in any way I could. I believe there were eighteen people in our community who never came home. The work we did together formed a bond and strengthened the idea that we were together in this. Volunteering and lending a hand not only provided me a sense of purpose, but it felt empowering to do something in an effort to take control of the situation. I needed to channel my feelings of anger and sorrow in a dignified, positive way.

It is critically important for all of us to pay attention to what is going on around the world and in our own backyard. We need to continue to support one another and remain courageous and fearless. I cannot stress enough that it is vitally important to encourage others to remain resilient and as tenacious as ever. We need to remain even more determined to never allow this act of hatred to define us or dictate how we should live our lives.

July: Tower of Remembrance at the Shrine of St. Joseph

JULY 11, 2002
THURSDAY: 10:30 a.m.

Today marked the ten-month anniversary of 9/11. Candles were lit and illuminated the victims' names on the board at the front of our room.

Our members opened the meeting with a commendation for a special man, Captain Robert Kumpf, of our local Basking Ridge Police Department. They presented Captain Kumpf with a Golden Eagle plaque for his outstanding dedication and support to the families of 9/11 in Basking Ridge. He had aided them in every way possible. Captain Kumpf was also a great source of strength for me. I thought of him as part of my team, and I often relied on his counsel and support. Captain Robert Kumpf's goodness will always be valiantly remembered.

After the presentation, I had the pleasure of introducing our next speaker. I began by telling our members that I met a lovely woman, Joanne, when I called the Shrine of Saint Joseph for some information. She was the sweet, soft-spoken woman at the front desk answering the calls that particular day. Sensitivity and a compassionate tone in her voice came through. This sweet lady offered to reach out to us in any way, so I began to ask her about herself. She told me that she was a Native American Indian. I asked her if she knew the ritual at the time of death for Native American Indians. When she replied that she did, I asked if she would consider coming in and sharing her story with our group. So, here she was!

Joanne opened by reading an Indian prayer. She had brought along a drum and a Native American dream catcher, which she shared with the group. In describing various Indian customs and rituals, Joanne mentioned the red-tailed hawk and how it played a spiritual role after death. In Indian lore, the hawk depicts strength and guidance and serves to protect Mother Earth from evil spirits. The hawk is also seen as a messenger, a purveyor of warnings, a symbol of protection, and possibly even the spirit of the deceased loved ones. Joanne had the group fully engaged. We thanked her for sharing her traditions with us, and we were grateful to this gentle woman who was filled with goodness and peace.

JULY 13, 2002
SUNDAY
THE DEDICATION OF THE TOWER OF REMEMBRANCE
THE SHRINE OF SAINT JOSEPH
STIRLING, NEW JERSEY

All was in place. The day had come for the dedication of this most awesome holy site, the bell tower at the Shrine of Saint Joseph in Stirling, New Jersey. All of our 9/11 families were invited, and most of them attended the ceremony. Since it was an ecumenical ceremony, clergy from all the churches in the area were present. Flowering plants and shrubs trimmed the perimeter of the steel towers. The Order of Service proceeded as follows:

    CALL FOR ASSEMBLY
    Bagpiper – Denis Donovan

WELCOME
Fr. Peter Krebs, S.T.

REFLECTIONS
Pam Koch, Laura Maler, Larry Hartman

SONG
"We Will Remember" sung by Carmel Boyle

BLESSING
Clergy

Father Peter Krebs blessed the Bell Tower:

GOD OF PEACE, *I stand before you asking for strength and courage for all who seek a world of reason and understanding.*

WELCOME HOME *the victims of September 11th; may they rest in your embrace and love.*

BY YOUR PRESENCE, *console and heal the families of these victims, lessening their agonizing pain.*

ALL LOVING GOD *ever attentive to your people, bless this Tower of Remembrance as a lasting memorial to those whose names are inscribed here. Bless, too, their loved ones in whose hearts their memories are forever enshrined.*

Magnify the goodwill and compassion that you planted within each of us at the moment of our creation, so that by our lives we might inspire hope and continue our work of building "THE CITY OF GOD."
Father Peter Krebs, S.T.

The Shrine of Saint Joseph

A MESSAGE OF HOPE
Presented by: Katy Soulas (9/11 family member)

Tolling of the Bells
Unveiling of the names were, the children of 9/11 victims:
Andrew Picarro, Timothy Soulas, Chris Reinig, Scott
Reinig, Alice Wisniewski, and Jonathan Wisniewski.

SONG
"God Bless America" sung by Carmel Boyle
Those present were invited to toll the bell if they wished to
do so. Refreshments followed.

Also included in the brochure prepared for the day:

May this Tower of Remembrance that we dedicate today
stand as a permanent memorial to all of the victims of the
terrorist attacks of 9/11/01 on the United States and Its
people. And safeguard humanity.

Music concluded the day.

Donated and created by Mr. Raymond Donovan, the bell tower
will always remain as a Sanctuary of Remembrance for all families
of 9/11. You have left your mark of goodness on the tablets of stone
and steel erected here, rising up to the heavens at the Shrine of Saint
Joseph. The bells will ring forth in memory of those who died on 9/11.
With deep appreciation in our hearts for you, Mr. Raymond Donovan,
thank you for your goodness, always.

I had learned that the four bells in this tower had originally been
located at the Seminary of the Missionary Servants of the Most Holy
Trinity in Monroe, Virginia. They had been blessed there and rang

there from 1960 until 1973 and had been silent since then. I noted to Mr. Donovan after the ceremony as we stood together under the tower, that the four bells had been given as a memorial to individuals who had died prior to 1960. The last bell closest to us was inscribed with the name of the person for whom it was given, "Raymond Koch." I pointed out to Ray that his name, Raymond, and my name, Koch, were inscribed on that bell! What were the chances of that happening?

REFLECTIONS FROM FATHER PETER KREBS

After the terrorists' attacks of 9/11, the question "Where is God?" was the primary concern of many people discussing with me their life's journey. This experience has given a new impetus to my priestly ministry.

I wanted to be able to respond to these people from my own encounter with God and not from something someone else experienced. The question was always so heartfelt. I wanted my response to be just as heartfelt. My response to, "Where is God?" had to come from my own questioning of God's presence in my life and my own discovery of that presence, a powerful contemplative journey. The experience of 9/11 brought my priestly ministry from my head to my heart.

August: Sunshine

AUGUST 1, 2002
THURSDAY: 10:30 a.m.
A SPECIAL GUEST

The setting for today's meeting was the glass room overlooking Harry Dunham Park. The sun shone brilliantly through the large windows all around us. I just loved this room!

We welcomed a young man, Robert Halligan from England, who lost his dad on 9/11. Robert came to the United States to share with us his transformative grief reaction through music. He is a singer and a songwriter, and a wonderful one at that. His song, "Sunshine" moved us all so deeply as he sang it while playing his guitar. I feel compelled to share these words with you with Robert's and his record company's permission:

SUNSHINE

Sunshine warm on my skin
Burning
And the rain falls, refreshing
But I am drowning
And I open my eyes and look for God,

but I'm blinded by the sun
I'm running
And the ground beneath is crumbling
And I am falling,
And all my world is falling with me
And I reach out my hand
And try to grasp
The truths I put aside
And I fall into your arms
I'm held near your heart
And I feel the power of love
With every beat I hear.
I fall into your arms
And I am lifted up
And the light of heaven's sun
Shines on me

I'm laughing
But inside my heart there's crying
And the tears that no one sees
Are falling
And I open my eyes and you see my pain
And you wipe it all away.

Blatant Promotions PPRS/MCPS

Robert also sang other songs he had written and joined us for lunch. It was a moving day uniting with our brother from the United Kingdom.

VACATION BREAK FOR THE REST OF AUGUST

One night in early August I was returning calls that had been made to our church. First, I wanted to put a call into Magical Beginnings, a business in Florida that I had researched to purchase butterflies from for our first anniversary 9/11 Memorial Mass of Remembrance. I had a vision for the 9/11 children releasing butterflies into the garden around the bell tower at the end of the Memorial Mass to mark the anniversary. For the amount of butterflies I needed, the cost was going to be $250. I thanked the man on the phone and told him I would have to think about it. Of the companies that I had researched, this one was the least expensive. Still, I really did not want to ask Monsignor for this money, as he had been so generous to me already, and it seemed a little extravagant.

I then proceeded to return the calls on my list. I dialed the first number, a young woman answered, and I explained who I was. She then told me she worked in one of the office buildings across the street from the World Trade Center. She said that she wanted to send a donation for $250 to the 9/11 families for the upcoming anniversary and asked if I could give her my address. "Wow!" I thought, and I thanked her for her kindness. I explained to her what her donation would be used for, and she was delighted. I hung up the phone and screamed, "Thank You, God!" There is no coincidence; God was with me every step of the way. It was blatantly obvious! Tears of joy ran down my face; I felt like we were so loved.

September: The First Anniversary

In early September, we received a letter from Mrs. Laura Bush, the First Lady of our nation. I had written to her when I started the group and asked her to visit us. Understandably, she was staying close to the White House and was not able to join us. She did not forget us, however. She sent a letter to our group as we approached the first anniversary. The families were touched deeply and were most grateful to Mrs. Bush for her thoughtfulness at this time. With permission from Mrs. Laura Bush, I am sharing her letter with you.

THE WHITE HOUSE
August 28, 2002

WTC Support Group
Church of Saint James
184 South Finley Avenue
Basking Ridge, New Jersey

Dear members of the WTC Support Group,
The work you are doing — the work of seeking healing
for yourselves and for each other – is a great gift you are
giving to your community and to America. That you are
coming together from different faiths and different cultures

to voice your pain and share your hope affirms the fact that if one human being hurts, all hurt; and if one gains strength, all become stronger.

President Bush and I ache for each of you as you go through the long days and months of loss. In our prayers, we ask that your sadness be lifted enough for life to have new meaning and that your memories be filled with the time that you had with your dear ones.

I hope that you continue to find sustaining strength in the bonds you are creating together.

With my deep sympathy and respect,

Laura Bush

Elise made copies of this letter on beautiful Crane's paper with the White House letterhead as keepsakes for each member of the group. We would hand these out at the next meeting on September 5.

SEPETEMBER 5, 2001
THURSDAY: 10:30 a.m.
"HOW TO GO ON"

I had invited two friends to speak today, both of whom had spoken to other groups that I had run. Bobby and Eileen Monetti are a dynamic couple, loving and warm individuals, who I knew would speak to the group's hearts. They had lost their son, Richard Paul Monetti, a student at Syracuse University, in *Flight 103* over Lockerbie, Scotland, on December 21, 1988. Both these parents were inspirational as they shared their story of their dear and beloved Rick's goodness. They have kept alive memories of their son and are activists in aiding the bereaved. We were touched deeply to know them, for they made us better people that day when they came to tell their story. We finished the session having lunch all together with Bobby and Eileen.

The second half of this meeting was an exercise. I had brought in my suitcase and placed it at the front of the room. I asked the group to explore what they would need to put in the suitcase in order to go forward. I asked them to write the ideas on a piece of paper and place them inside the carryall. Words of — patience, courage, strength, endurance, etc. would be appropriate. All were good qualities to carry with them, and many more ideas were added to the suitcase. A beneficial exercise indeed!

SEPTEMBER 6, 2002
FRIDAY: 1:00 p.m.
"MEDIA DAY" ~ APPROACHING THE FIRST ANNIVERSARY

The first anniversary was approaching quickly, and we had been preparing for months. Leading up to this date, the media was calling the church daily. I decided that I would invite all members of the media who had called to come to our room for a "Media Day." My desire was to explain to the newspaper and TV reporters, as well as to the Diocese of Metuchen publicity team member, what these families were going through. I also invited any of our group members who wanted to be present with me to attend. Only four of our members attended; all others present were from the media.

I welcomed everyone and shared how the families were in a state of anticipatory grief. I conveyed to the press that these families were reliving the days leading up to the horrific event of a year ago. The emotions and feelings of a deep traumatic complicated grief reaction were resurfacing. It was a very painful time for them. I mentioned that they were fragile and delicate, and we must respect them in the gentlest of ways in their grief. I told the media that we had asked the families to turn off their TV's and avoid newspapers and magazines as much as they could, especially for the sake of the children. I had suggested to the families that they seek out age-appropriate movies for their children to view on that day. Most of the families wanted to be together so they could memorialize their lost loved ones in private.

One family member present then spoke and made comments. I asked for questions from the media, and we concluded for the day. I observed that the media was extremely respectful.

The week leading up to the first anniversary was a frenetic time for our group. Many of the families had relatives arriving from out of town. I had been to meetings with the mayor, the police, and town officials. I also met with the volunteers, who were working so hard to plan for the first anniversary. There were many details to tie up for the coming 9/11 Memorial Mass at the Shrine of Saint Joseph. We reviewed one last time our list of readers, the offertory procession, the songs, the butterflies, and the physical set up.

Saint James Church sits on South Finley Avenue, which runs into the center of Basking Ridge. In collaboration with the police and other surrounding churches, a decision was made to invite townspeople to join us in lining South Finley Avenue with luminaries on the anniversary evening of 9/11. The invitation would be announced at all our masses and church services. Elise and I made plans to split up and speak at the masses at Saint James to put the word out.

Our group's secretary, Prudence Pigott, arranged for local newspapers to run a page with the message of *Grateful Appreciation* for the many businesses whose support had been invaluable over the year for the 9/11 families. The list was lengthy, and the outreach was amazing to see on paper.

SEPTEMBER 10, 2002
TUESDAY: 10:30 a.m.

In anticipation of the anniversary the following day, we hosted an open house in our room at Saint James Church. Not many people came, but some did, and it was important to be available at this time.

SEPTEMBER 11, 2002
WEDNESDAY: 7:45 a.m.
ATTENDANCE APPROXIMATELY 500-550
THE FIRST ANNIVERSARY OF SEPTEMBER 11, 2001
THE 9/11 MEMORIAL MASS OF REMEMBRANCE

The dreaded day was here, the first anniversary of 9/11, that oh so horrific day. I cannot stress how much we wanted privacy to mourn at this sacred time. For this reason, we chose not to publicize this memorial out of the respect for the families. I imagined the members of the group reliving each hour of the year prior to this day in their minds and hearts, feelings resurfacing, and the media opening up those painful wounds all over again. The majority of the families in our group wanted to be together for the first anniversary, and that we were. Only a few families elected to go to Ground Zero in New York City.

At 7:45 a.m., I pulled into the parking lot at the Shrine of Saint Joseph in Stirling, New Jersey. Already the lot was filling up. Police and shrine members were directing the traffic into parking spaces. The sun shone brightly upon us, and there was hardly a cloud in the sky. I flashed back to the tragic day a year earlier. The fresh scent of evergreens filled the air; birds were chirping in the trees. This was a sanctuary of serenity, I thought, as I approached the sacred space nestled in the tall pine trees before me. Into my vision came the illustrious bell tower, rising high toward the heavens. Brilliant yellow chrysanthemums graced the perimeter of the tower. The area bustled with activity. On the walking path, greeters were handing out brochures. Copies of a book of prayers and poems were piled high on a table and being handed out to the children of 9/11. The book, titled, *Together,* had been written and created by the children of the Saint Joseph School in Mendham, New Jersey. How kind of our friends at Saint Joseph School to think of us on this day. What an unexpected surprise that made us feel so loved and comforted.

One last time I went over it all in my head. It looked as though all was in place. My eye was instantly drawn to the focal point, the altar, set at the center of the bell tower in a place for all to see. It was draped in a white tablecloth with two lit candles, one on either side. In front of the altar sat several large boxes also draped in white cloths, on top of which stood seventy-six tall white glass votive candles. These would be used for our opening candle lighting. We then would flow into the 9/11 Memorial Mass of Remembrance. The theme, "We Will Remember," mirrored the chant written and would be sung by Carmel Boyle, a friend of the Shrine from Ireland. Close to the altar was a small table with the offertory gifts, including the Chalice and the Paten that our group had made on December 6, 2001, in our program, with the guiding hands of the potter, Ray Boswell. They were his gift to our group. All the planning had come to fruition.

Being present at this sacred place seemed so right and fitting on this somber day. This was a peaceful space of healing and prayer. People gathered by the names of their loved ones, raised in bronze from the panels on the memorial walls surrounding the tower. Families were hugging one another. The music ministers, Matthew Hagovsky and Marion Drew, were present. I observed what had to be at least 500–550 people gathered, including police and fire departments from the area.

At 8:15 we began. I stood to welcome the people and gave a short talk thanking those who helped make this day possible. I also thanked most especially, Mr. Raymond Donovan for creating and erecting the bell tower. I thanked the Shrine of Saint Joseph for warmly welcoming us as a group. I thanked the music ministers and the sound engineers. I then mentioned the order of the day including the candle lighting as well as protocol for when the bells would toll, and for the releasing of the butterflies after the 9/11 Memorial Mass of Remembrance.

After a slight pause, I said, "We now will begin the candle-lighting ceremony of light and love."

Marion began playing the soft, familiar instrumental music by Paul Alexander, "Light a Candle," and I called forth the designated member of each 9/11 family present to light their candles. I intermittently read, the Litany of Remembrance, *We Remember Them*, (from the Gates of Repentance: the New Union Prayer Book of Awe) during the candle lighting. After the prayer was over, Marion Drew and Matthew Hagovsky joined in singing, "Light a Candle." The entire ritual was moving, impressive, and beautiful to witness.

After the candles were completely lit, we held a slight pause for reflection. Then, once again music began, and the Celebrant and Concelebrants processed down the path. Beautiful moving chant-like song entitled, "We Will Remember" was sung by Carmel Boyle, she helped to soothe our weary souls.

Father Peter Krebs opened the 9/11 Memorial Mass of Remembrance: "In the Name of the Father and of His Son and of His Holy Spirit. Amen." He then welcomed the people, and he acknowledged the Concelebrants and thanked them for joining us. He proceeded with a heartfelt prayer.

Suddenly at 8:46 a.m., the bells tolled, a stunning and piercing sound that permeated to the very core of our beings. It was at this moment when the first plane, United Airlines Flight 11, hits into the North Tower of the World Trade Center. We paused for a moment of silence to remember those who died. Tears began to flow; crying could be heard and sniffling all around. Father Peter continued the mass. Then at 9:03 a.m., the bells tolled again, a reminder of the second plane, United Airlines Flight 175, hitting the South Tower of the World Trade Center. We all paused.

At this moment, a terrific swirling wind came over us, and many of the candles that were lit were blown out. Above us, three red-tailed hawks circled around us! What a powerful moment! Several of the group members were standing around me as we looked up into the sky, then at each other. Our eyes instantly filled with tears. We held tightly together for a long moment. We all flashed back to Joanne's presentation on Native American Indian rituals, given exactly two months earlier to our group. Joanne had mentioned that in Indian lore the red-tailed hawk is believed to play a role at the time of death. For the families of 9/11, the spirits of their deceased loved ones were with them; this was a sign that confirmed it. They were with us protecting them on this day, and of that we were sure. I myself have witnessed the red-tailed hawk several times at graveside burials.

A family member now read the first scripture text, and then the psalm was sung. A 9/11 family member moved to the podium to deliver the second reading. During Monsignor Capik's reading of the gospel and powerful homily with a message of hope, the bells began to toll once again at 9:37 a.m., for those who died in *American Airlines Flight 77* at the Pentagon. All of us remained motionless and prayerful.

The Prayers of the Faithful followed Monsignor's homily, and they were read by one of our group members. The offerings, for the offertory, flowed down the path. This was led by our police officer, Captain Robert Kumpf, holding over his head the *New York Times: Portraits of Grief*. Many of our 104 children of the 9/11 victims followed, holding flowers that they would place under the bell tower, a most touching sight to behold. Communion was served and continued on for a lengthy time, as there were so many people present. After communion, meditative poems were read, and a 9/11 family member gave a talk on her feelings about the day. Her words were so moving and heartfelt, and they deeply touched us. Beautiful music such as, "The Prayer" and "You Raise Me Up" were woven into this memorial. At 10:07 a.m., the bells tolled a fourth time. This time they were for the victims of *United Airlines Flight 93* who died in Shanksville, Pennsylvania.

Father Peter concluded the memorial with a meaningful blessing. After the ending song of, "God Bless America," Father instructed the people present to come forward and strike the bell with the mallet. He then requested the families to say the names of their deceased loved one into the microphone. I directed the children to come forward and receive an envelope with a butterfly inside. The children would then release the butterflies into the gardens around the bell tower.

With each strike of the mallet, the sound of the bell rang out. There was hugging and holding among family and friends. In the garden, butterflies flitted from flower to flower. It was a somber time, but an oh-so-heartfelt and dignified homage paid to the victims of 9/11.

A brunch followed in the auditorium at Saint James Church. Our volunteers extended a warm welcome to our families and their relatives, giving hugs all around. It had been a long, hard morning. Children from the Saint James School had decorated the auditorium stage with an abundant collection of cards, and volunteers had placed pictures of our group among the cards. Long tables filled the room, covered with white tablecloths and beautiful floral centerpieces. Around the perimeter, several white-skirted serving tables held an abundance of enticing foods of every kind. An assortment of beverages was set up in another section. I arrived late to the brunch because I had attended a burial at the nearby Episcopal Church with one of the families.

Later in the evening, Monsignor said mass once again for the Saint James Church, and several 9/11 families and parishioners attended. At this same time, I was giving a talk at the Shrine of Saint Joseph at their candlelight prayer service. I then proceeded over to join Monsignor and other religious leaders in front of the Basking Ridge Town Hall where townspeople had assembled for another candlelight prayer service. Monsignor, as well as other members of the clergy, delivered words of consolation and solace. I gave a message of thanksgiving to the townspeople who reached out to our support group during the year, promoting healing for the families of 9/11.

The town was aglow with luminaries lining South Finley Avenue. We walked to our cars afterward, feeling proud to be Americans who lived in this caring town of Basking Ridge, filled with so much goodness. But, we were sad at the loss of our beautiful treasured victims and the families that endured such suffering and pain.

At the end of a full day, it was now time to pamper us.

SEPTEMBER 12, 2002
THURSDAY: 10:30 a.m.
10 in attendance
OPEN HOUSE

We had an open house the following day for the group or anyone who needed to vent and discuss the anniversary. Refreshments were available. Only a small group attended.

SEPTEMBER 19, 2002
THURSDAY: 10:30 a.m.
(20- in attendance)

We had low attendance numbers for the discussion day about the first anniversary and the 9/11 Memorial Mass of Remembrance. I also had planned a pep rally for "The Bear Makin' Bikin Ladies." They were about to set off for their bike trip from Ground Zero to Washington, DC. We enjoyed some refreshments together and wished them well. As a small token of our appreciation, we presented them with the gift of pale pink t-shirts. On one side of the t-shirt were the words, **The Saint James 9/11 Bereavement Support Group Basking Ridge, N.J.** On the other side was written, **The Bear Makin' Bikin' Ladies.**

We toasted them with sparkling cider: "You are an inspiration to all of us and you will always be a part of us! Your goodness and your tribute shall forever be remembered. We pray for a safe trip."

SEPTEMBER 26, 2002
THURSDAY: 10:30 a.m.
WHERE DO WE GO FROM HERE?

We were still meeting, though our numbers had dropped considerably after the first anniversary. Many members wanted to continue, but I was mindful of the volunteers and was thinking of scaling down. Most of the volunteers, if asked, would have stuck by us, but they had lives of their own, and I did not want to take advantage of their goodness. The babysitters were steadfast with us, as was our hospitality team, but on a lesser level.

We agreed we would meet every other week, at our same time on the same day. I planned to continue with guest speakers and add social events out of the room, in, place of a meeting. I wanted the group to elect a chairperson and a co-chairperson who would help keep the group connected. I asked them to think about it for the next couple of weeks and then we would vote.

Sharing information remained important. The families still needed to work on how to aid their children, as well as manage their paperwork. Many were still attending appointments with their one-on-one therapists, and several children were also getting aid. The group members were close to their buddy's.

I suggested that we patronize the businesses that had supported the group during its first year. Another suggestion was to form a luncheon group to frequent The Madison Hotel, as well as other surrounding restaurants that had reached out to us.

REFLECTIONS FROM LAURIE SUMMERS, A BEAR MAKIN' LADY

We as "The Bear Makin' Ladies" were so grateful that we could do something that brought some comfort to the families of 9/11 victims. We learned after giving the first round of bears, what the power of receiving felt like. We realized that receiving and accepting a gift is as powerful and maybe more so than the giving of it. We were overwhelmed with the thanks we got from the families. Here we are fifteen years after 9/11, and we are still making bears!

We probably have made nearly 2,000 bears since 9/11. We do it by word of mouth. We also make bears for "Good Grief," a group that helps children, teens, young adults, and their families cope with the grief of losing a parent or a sibling. Through the formation of "The Bear Makin' Ladies," it helped us grieve and process our emotions of 9/11. We were directly and indirectly affected by this tragedy. Making these bears together allowed us to talk and cry and share our emotions of this event. Unknowingly, we were supporting each other and helping each other move through our grief. Also, as a result of reaching out to the victim's families, and trying to help them through the bears, we have found that we have formed a friendship with each other that is deep and real. It is a comfort to know we will have these friendships forever.

Later, "The Bear Makin' Bikin' Ladies" was formed, and we rode our bikes (with 3,000 other bikers) from New York City to Washington, DC.

"For all of us, when we thought we could not pedal anymore, we thought of the families of 9/11 …if they could get up each day and live that day, we could certainly find the strength to pedal more miles. We all pedaled every mile."

Mary Ellen Peters, Kris Koop, Nancy Lechleider, Marianne Pawlicki, Michelle Reedy, Chris Pape, Gindy McCarthy and Laurie Summers were the "The Bear Makin' Bikin' Ladies." Chris overcame health challenges and rode the first twenty miles with us.

Joan Dill and her husband Tom volunteered throughout the whole ride (three days from NYC to Washington, DC.) They worked the rest stops and set up our tents each night for us, washed our bike clothes, and had goodies for us! Just amazing!

How has this experience changed my life? It has empowered me to trust in my inner voice to let someone who is hurting know that I am thinking of him or her and sending a hug. I have learned to trust in the power of small kindnesses, and I have learned to become a more empathetic person.

The power of the bears we make still amazes me. One story that touched our hearts is about a five-year-old boy who lost his dad on 9/11. He had not slept through a night until he received his bear made out of his dad's shirt. He was then able to sleep at night, hugging his bear.

Chapter 25

The Second Year

OCTOBER 10, 2002
THURSDAY: 10:30 a.m.
CHILDREN AND GRIEF REVISITED

One day, I received a call from Donna Gaffney of Summit, New Jersey. She was a child trauma specialist with an impressive background. She asked if she might be of some help, and after a couple of phone conversations, we set a date for her to come speak with the families. Today was the day. Her demeanor was calm with her empathy and sympathy shining through. Donna was so good and such a valuable resource for the group that I planned to invite her back another time.

We voted for the new chairperson and co-chairperson to help the group stay connected. They would also aid me as we weaned the group. Empowering and enabling was crucial.

OCTOBER 25, 2002
FRIDAY: 11:00 a.m.
A DAY OF RENEWAL

An invitation to the Shrine gave us a lovely day of spiritual enrichment and renewal hosted by Father Peter and his team to comfort my team.

"A beautiful sight to behold," I thought as I walked into the large gathering room early on this morning. The gathering room was a blissful place with large picture windows overlooking a panoramic view of colorful fall trees skirting the lush green park-like setting before us. I enjoyed the peace and serenity, as did all who attended this day.

NOVEMBER 14, 2002
THURSDAY: 10:30 a.m.
THANKSGIVING APPROACHING / "TUESDAY'S CHILDREN"

The Thanksgiving holiday was on the way, and it was time for us to give thanks. I wanted to recognize Father Peter Krebs and Pat Hughes for coddling all of us through this difficult time. At a prior meeting, I had asked for a volunteer to present a gift, and hands had shot up. I selected one of the girls, and she wrote a beautiful tribute. Today she delivered her tribute to Father Peter and Pat and presented them with a silver Loving Cup, an appropriate gift that expressed our gratitude for these two people. We thanked them and toasted them with sparkling cider. I myself recognized them as catalysts for the Divine Healer, as they helped to point us in the direction of healing itself.

DECEMBER 5, 2002
THURSDAY: 10:30 a.m.
"THE SEVEN HABITS..."

I opened the day with prayer and breathing techniques. Today I wanted to touch on, **The 7 Habits of Highly Effective People in Grief,** which I had adapted from Stephen Covey's book, *The 7 Habits of Highly Effective People.* (I love this book! I think it is a good rule of thumb for all people to read, not only those in the corporate field, but those in many roles in life who could apply it as well. I have always thought of this book as a valuable tool for teens as well as adults. If we all could live by the order of these thoughts, we could generate a more peaceful world.)

After a break for refreshments, the second segment of the day featured a speaker from the non-profit service organization, "Tuesday's Children." This organization reached out to our 9/11 children with events and activities of all kinds, such as tickets to sports games, shows, and various events that helped foster healthy child development. Tuesday's Children was created in conjunction with New York University's Child Study Center. Many of the children from our group benefited from this organization.

DECEMBER 19, 2002
THURSDAY: 10:30 a.m.
A CHRISTMAS BRUNCH

Our co-chairperson, Susan, invited us all to a Christmas brunch at her warm and beautiful home. It was a lovely gathering with a light-hearted Christmas spirit all around us.

At this time, I stopped journaling about the group. I am not really sure why, but with the Thanksgiving and Christmas holidays, I just got away from it. I recall we continued our meetings every other week until June 2003 when we broke for the summer months. Among the programs that I recall was the librarian from the Basking Ridge library talking about researching a family tree, Donna Gaffney came back to talk on the topic of, "Special Issues for Children in Traumatic Grief," and representatives of grief camps coming to present their programs to us.

FEBRUARY 2003
AN UNEXPECTED HONOR FROM SOMERSET COUNTY

I received a letter in the mail one day in February. I was being invited to an annual dinner with the Somerset County Commission on the Status of Women. They had selected me to receive an Outstanding Women in Somerset County Award for my work with the group. (I learned later that the 9/11 families had nominated me.) After reading the letter, my head dropped into my hands and my eyes instantly filled with tears.

"This honor is all yours, oh God," I thought. "It was 'You' shining through us," I prayed at this quiet moment. I only wished that we could all recognize that the kingdom of God was within all of us; surely it was in each and every one of my co-workers and volunteers. What a more peaceful world this would be if we kept this in mind.

Many members of my team, as well as members of our group, attended the awards dinner. It was a lovely affair, but I could not accept the award alone since there were so many who worked alongside me. All on our team — women and men — were outstanding individuals. This award was for all of us. When I got up to accept the award, I introduced Monsignor Capik and showered him with many accolades. I recognized him as my right arm, and I then asked him to come stand next to me on my right. I then asked Elise to join me at the podium on my left. I introduced Elise as my left arm and bestowed many compliments on her. Next, I asked the grief facilitators to stand behind me. I then asked the families to come forward and stand behind the facilitators. They were reluctant at first, but with encouragement, they moved forward slowly.

I was now surrounded by many of our group at the podium. I felt so much better with them all around me. I asked them to join hands and raise their arms high to the heavens to where the victims were. We would all dedicate this award to them.

I spoke loudly, "It is in YOUR names, the victims of 9/11, that we stand here tonight and dedicate this award to YOU. We make YOU a solemn promise on this memorable occasion together that YOU will never be forgotten. YOU will be carried in our hearts forever and YOU will always be remembered for all of your goodness. AMEN."

My voice held a strong conviction for each and every word, the likes of which I had never recognized in myself before. This dedication was a moving end to the evening. Tears could be seen in all of the eyes around me.

JUNE 5, 2003
THURSDAY: 10:30 a.m.
A SPECIAL GUEST

For our last meeting before summer, we gathered again in the glass room at Harry Dunham Park. Bright sunlight filled the room on what would be a memorable day. As we looked out over the grounds of the park, the flagpole was in sight with the flag flying high against the blue sky above.

Our guest for the day was a naval airman John, whom our group had adopted as an email pal while he was deployed in Iraq. The group had written him letters of support and thanksgiving and had sent prayers for his safety. Today, we would meet him for the first time to welcome him home.

When he arrived, we thanked him over and over for his service. He replied, "I feel very unworthy to have these thanks given to me."

The young man told us that he had answered every email, and he told us of his gratitude. On his birthday alone, he received more than one hundred emails. It was a wholehearted celebration this day to have him back home in the USA!

After indulging in lunch and a, patriotic "welcome home" cake, as well as light conversation and photo ops, we stepped outside and moved toward the prominent flagpole. We stood hand-in-hand for a reading of a prayer of thanksgiving for this naval airman's safe return. Yellow balloons were released into the sky. It was surely a special day for all of us there present.

JULY 2003

The summer months went by so quickly. I spent my time in Chatham, Massachusetts on Cape Cod. We had purchased a small house there shortly after 9/11 to build memories with our family. I enjoyed the sand and the sea, but the families of 9/11 never strayed far from my heart and thoughts. I was planning the memorial liturgy for the second anniversary. I was looking for a theme while sitting on the picturesque Andrew Harding's Beach, with the gifts of early morning light and the glistening blue waters before me. Fishing boats were passing by and followed by echoing seagulls. A short distance away, seals lay perched in the sun on the sandbars of North Beach and the Atlantic, an inspiring haven indeed. "Now here is a great place to go to work!" I thought.

AUGUST 2003

My daughter Jessica and her college friends from the University of Virginia made a visit to the Cape. One day, they coaxed me into joining them on a jaunt to Nantucket. It did not take much to twist my arm; I love to visit this quaint and magical jewel by the sea. We rented bikes and rode them on the bike path loop out to Sconset. On the ride back, I found myself having to stop often from fatigue, maybe eight times or so. I sent the girls ahead of me, but I did finish the ride. The girls all clapped and cheered at the sight of me reaching the end of the bike path. I had made it!

SEPTEMBER 2003

In early September, I returned to New Jersey to tie up loose ends for the second Memorial Mass of Remembrance. All was in place for the day. Our group's chairperson and co-chairperson helped immensely in preparing for the day. A kind invitation was sent to everyone in the group for a brunch at a group member's home the day before the 9/11 Memorial Mass of Remembrance. The gathering was a good time of being together on a lighter note.

SEPTEMBER 11, 2003

We could hardly believe it, but the second anniversary had arrived. Just like the prior year, the day dawned clear and sunny. The 9/11 Memorial

Mass of Remembrance around the bell tower was well attended, and it was moving and emotional. We were grateful to have the music ministers with us, along with Father Peter and Monsignor Capik.

This year, Father Giles from the Benedictine order concelebrated the mass. He had lost a relative, and coincidentally a mutual friend of Bob and mine, Frank Skidmore in the World Trade Center on 9/11. This was a somber time, and all the feelings began resurfacing for the families. The liturgy was meaningful. For the candle-lighting ceremony, the parents who had lost children were asked to light the candles. It was extremely moving.

We kept to the same order of service as the original year, but we changed the theme of the day to "The Lighthouse of Hope," and the readings were most appropriate. We stood upon this holy ground once more at the Shrine of Saint Joseph with a lighthouse in sight constructed of wood in front of the altar as the symbol for hope and light in the darkness. For many more years to come, we would be there, I was sure. It was truly a place of serenity, and right and just to be there.

Unlike the prior year, the candles stayed lit, but it was still sad and solemn as the names were announced and the bell was struck over and over with the mallet. I hugged many of the familiar families one more time. I noticed that the children were getting older, but still, the pain was very much present. After the memorial, many of the families joined with relatives at home.

A Frightful Diagnosis

In the month following the second anniversary, I worked on many menial jobs around the house and then I started to notice black and blue marks on my legs. I instantly thought of leukemia. I made an appointment to see my oncologist, Dr. Dan Moriarty. The day of my appointment, I had lunch beforehand with my friend in Chatham. While in conversation with Cheryl, I realized my head would just drop. I left and proceeded to Overlook Hospital, where Doctor Moriarty's office was located. During the visit, I was told my platelets were 400 instead of 400,000. Dr. Dan had been called out of his office, so another doctor who was covering for him, told me I could not leave and that I needed to have a blood transfusion immediately.

My life changed in the spin of a dime. The world stopped, and it felt as though the wind had been knocked out of me. A couple of days later I met with Dr. Dan, who told me more testing was needed.

Then came the frightful day. I had been diagnosed with a blood cancer called Acute Myelogenous Leukemia (AML). The medicine protocol I had taken for breast cancer treatment had a ninety-seven percent cure rate, but a one percent chance of giving me leukemia. I had taken the risk, and now I had become the one percent!

I was fifty-four years old when diagnosed with AML. I wanted to learn if I had any hope at all and if I should even fight. I knew it would be hard to fight this disease. I was so drained from the grief of knowing that I had AML, but I thought life was just too precious not to fight. So, I set my mind to be proactive. I began with the end in mind, which would be more life and living it. God would be my partner and guide me in each decision I would have to make. What better hands could I ever be in? I would do first things first, just like in *The 7 Habits….*

I wanted to write letters to my husband and each of my children. Tearfully and excruciatingly, I sat down at the computer for the daunting task at hand. "What document name do I put this under," I thought. And then it came to me: "The Truffles of My Life." My beautiful family was truly the ultimate sweetness of life for me, and so I began with tears uncontrollably rolling down my face. In full emotion with each word, I wrote to those beautiful faces I loved so dearly. I was truly questioning if I could survive. Grueling mental agony lay heavy on my spirit. A dark time it was indeed.

I had worked for hospice for thirteen years. Following my training, I had devoted much of my free time to the terminally ill patients while my children were in school. It was a calling that the Lord passed along to me after my sister Joan had died. For me, it was a privilege being with the hospice patient, as well as the family, in this intimate and sacred time at the end of life. I was listening all the time and hearing many of their life stories, which were precious gems and just treasures beyond gold. These patients were gifts to me.

Now the psychological challenge for me was to disconnect from thinking I was the dying patient and fight for the cure for the person who I was. The trajectory of my thoughts was changing often, and combating these dark feelings was difficult. I needed a plan of action. Whenever I found myself in this dark space, I developed a mantra and would say to myself: "That is not you, Pam. You are not there." I would say it out loud, over and over again. I would then change my physical location into the light. I would go for a walk or look at the garden outside my window. I read magazines, listened to soft music, and watched funny movies.

The knowledge of having a life-threatening illness, such as leukemia, was so much more than I ever could have even imagined. I was all consumed by it, and it seemed to be the most immobilizing force that I had ever experienced. I was in an uncertain time of my life for sure.

Bridge over Troubled Waters

My life had been a journey filled with many happy and joyful days, days of loving and days of goodness. I had also experienced sad days, hard dark days of loss, days to make choices, and days to take risks.

After one of those dark days of loss, I experienced a dream-like imagery where I envisioned myself actually walking along a path in the woods under a big bridge. Before me, I saw sets of stepping stones, leading in different directions. Putting my trust in God, I became the risk taker and stepped forward onto the stones leading to "hospice". Farther along the path forked, and I went right, alongside a river, onto a path marked, "Bereavement Ministry". I came to know it as a road to liberation, growth, and transformation. This road was leading into a valley called "Living with Cancer". I thought I knew a lot about this valley, even after working in the field for thirteen years, I realized I had so much more to learn when walking in the shoes of a cancer patient. It was here in this foreign land called, "Breast Cancer", I had encountered an avalanche of love surrounding me so profoundly. This outpouring of love, I concluded, was the "gift" of this horrendous disease.

I pressed on through this valley, hiking over some very steep hills until I found a path marked, "Beyond Breast Cancer." I had traveled only a short distance on this path when I came upon an enormous storm known as "9/11," the likes of which I, and many others, had never seen before. The ramifications were unimaginable for all affected. The rushing waters flooded the path and triggered a large waterfall called, "Tears." The thunderstorm of "Grief" lingered on for a very long time. The water rose high. Many had to battle the strong currents to stay afloat. Suddenly, on the jagged rocks up on the Bluff of Saint James, there came into view, lighthouses of many sizes and shapes, lighting a path to hope and goodness.

And then, I returned slowly to reality, back into the room where I lay in my bed. I opened my eyes to go forward in the fight for my life against my nemesis AML, that sword of *Damocles* hanging over me. I identified my path as rocky and a life-threatening one. If I ever had the chance for more life, I was to recognize that the mighty bridge over the troubled waters was God, my creator, and so I handed over to God what was God's.

At that moment I opted to focus on the days of goodness and light, happy days that were carefree and loving, of which there were many. I put into the forefront of my mind my marriage to Bob, the birth of our children, whom I adored, and my grandchildren, for whom I had great hope.

Plan of Action: Fighting for the Cure Once Again

D r. Dan sent me to Robert Wood Johnson Hospital in New Brunswick, New Jersey, to see a specialist, Dr. Strair. After my examination, he admitted me right from his office into a hospital room and began treatment immediately to put me into remission. The doctor told me that I would be in the hospital for thirty days. It was a very emotional time for Bob and me.

My room on the bone marrow floor was clean and stark. A nurse handed me a light blue gown. She said that I could put on the walls anything that I would like. I was thinking of a focal point to try to center myself; I was such a mess. The nurse said she would do it for me. She told me to pick any color of masking tape; she had them all. I picked green for the color of hope. I described to her The Pax-Christi symbol and she knew it and created it for me about 4' tall. I thought breast cancer was difficult, but leukemia seemed to be a whole lot worse. At 4 a.m. each morning my blood would be tested; I had truly become a human pincushion. The many bone marrow aspirates were even tougher.

One day the nurse entered my room with a stack of mail. She asked me who I was, and I told her I was Pam Koch, just a simple person.

She exclaimed, "You received thirty-eight cards today, and we don't usually get so many at a time here."

"Well," I said, "I am a simple person who was blessed with many friends."

The following day a wonderful surprise came my way. Suzie Sullivan, one of my dear friends, had a daughter, Molly, who was a nurse. Molly appeared in my room and said that she worked on the bone marrow floor where I was located. "It seems Dr. Moriarty was a smart planner," I thought! Molly came often to visit me. She was such a warm piece of home whom I so eagerly welcomed. Molly was truly like flannel to my heart! Her terrific mom, Suzie, made me my favorite mint brownies, and she and another mutual friend, Charlene Larkin, organized a quilt-making group of my friends from Chatham. Molly came in one day with their beautifully created quilt, bearing the names of a friend on each square. I instantly put this cherished possession over me as the tears flowed down my face. This was a treasure I will always hold dear. I recognized goodness was all around me.

The 9/11 families walked alongside me every step of the way. Artwork from the 9/11 children came in the mail daily. The wall before me that had once been stark was beginning to look like an art gallery. Adorning that wall were drawings of all kinds — horses, family stick figures in crayon on bright pieces of paper, and beautiful bunches of colorful flowers. I did not know it at the time, but the 9/11 girls were hard at work in the basement of our group's chairperson's home creating a scrapbook about the group for me. Letters and cards flowed daily from all the families. Monsignor Capik came to visit me and anointed me with the Sacrament of the Sick. Some of the group families came, but hospital personnel would not allow them into my hospital room. It was strictly immediate family only. I felt sad not to greet the families. On November 14, 2003, my daughter Kerry gave birth to our first grandchild. I was so distraught not to be with her at this very special time that every grandmother looks forward to with joyful enthusiasm. My, son-in-law Barry, came to my hospital room that night to share a video he made of Grace's birth. She was magnificent and as sweet as could be. Grace Pamela was the best medicine of all!

Finally after thirty days, I was going home, and the hardest time was over, I thought. I was so eager to meet my darling new granddaughter, Grace Pamela Gilrane, for the first time. I just could not wait! My dear friend, Maris, had sent me a soft pink top with pink feathery trim around the neck to wear when holding Grace for the first time. The medical staff was amazed I did not need a wheelchair to leave the hospital. I just walked out of the building. I had constantly walked up and down the halls, as directed by the nurses, and it had paid off. Most people on my ward could never have walked out of the building, on their own.

I felt anxious as the car pulled into my driveway and I walked through our familiar doors. Kerry and baby Grace greeted me at the entrance of the family room. Smiles burst from ear to ear on my face, and euphoria filled my heart. This was truly better than Christmas! I then went and sat on our yellow family room couch, and Kerry placed Grace into my arms. I held her up against my cheek, her skin so soft, and her scent so sweet. This was a familiar scent her own mother had when she was an infant, I thought. Grace was dressed in a pink onesie with lambs embroidered all over it. Her rosy round cheeks, black wisps of hair, and big blue eyes lead me to be enamored by this angelic cherub! While gazing at this little Irish beauty, lying in my arms, tears of joy and thanksgiving spilled over from my eyes.

I was home for only a short time, maybe a few days, when the infections started. I started to make frequent trips to the hospital. I did not even have to check-in anymore. I would just go immediately to the floor and be put into a bed and instantly hooked up to an IV. On my third visit back, I called my sisters to say goodbye. I was sure I would not survive this time. My fever was high — 103 degrees. Delirium started, and I struggled to breathe. I then lapsed into a coma.

My family called our dear friend, Father Paddy O'Donovan, to come to Robert Woods Johnson Hospital in New Brunswick, New Jersey. He arrived after a terrible snowstorm. Kerry and Barry and infant Grace were staying in a nearby hotel. When I heard my daughter's voice telling me that Father Paddy was there, I opened my eyes for just a moment. The room was black around me, and Father Paddy's face was illuminated, a light shining all around his head. I took my hands from under the covers and put my palms up, ready for him to carry out the anointing of the sick. Then I faded back into the coma. I was in a place of total tranquility, where there was no pain and no cancer on my mind, only sheer peacefulness. I just wanted to stay in this state. For three days I was there. Two weeks later I learned that my fever at that time had been heading toward 108 degrees. To bring the fever down, I was submerged in a tub of ice. I have no memory of this whatsoever.

The 9/11 families learned I was in a critical situation. They asked Monsignor Capik to say a healing mass for me that night. The group members and facilitators invited several of our friends to join them at the mass.

The next morning I opened my eyes and I could hear Kerry yell across to the nurses station, She's up!" I had come out of the coma. Later in the day the doctors came into the room and mentioned I had a little fluid in my left lung that they wanted to remove. I was familiar with this procedure from my hospice work, and I was not too keen on it. The Pastoral Care nun, who had come to visit me often, happened to come into my room right after the team of doctors had left. She talked me right into the treatment.

The next morning, a medical team took me down to the procedure room where they positioned me next to a sterile tray on which was placed the long sterile needle. I can remember talking to God, saying, "Into Your hands, I commend my spirit."

Using a sonogram, a technician looked at my lung to see where to insert the needle. Seconds later, she said, "The fluid is gone... there is no need for the procedure"!

The healing prayers of the 9/11 families were heard! Bringing me out of the coma and then having the fluid in the lung disappear were the very first two miracles performed by the 9/11 families. I had so much faith in this group I predicted more miracles from them in the days ahead for the many others they would meet in life. Oh, those 9/11 families, we must have done something right, I told myself. They were now strong enough to give back, and they did it with all their might. This group was now keeping me afloat.

My daughter, Jessica, had left her job to escort me to all my appointments. I do not know what I would have done without her. To this day, I remain most grateful to her for the sacrifice she made in caring for me. I was becoming well enough to be more mobile, but not able to go into crowds. My numbers were stabilizing, and I was functioning.

The next step was an appointment at Memorial Sloan Kettering Cancer Center to meet with Dr. Ann Jakubowski, a hematologist whom Doctor Strair had referred me to. Dr. Ann Jakubowski would head up my team for a T cell Transplant. How blessed I was when I met up with this woman of excellence! I was even more blessed when she found me a donor in the donor bank. I thought about all the people who had never found a donor and had died waiting for one. I thought, too, of the elderly and the little children who were dealing with what I was experiencing. It was all so heartbreaking to me. I was in a very dark place, yet the news that a donor was found for me gave me a ray of hope.

In earlier days, while working at Saint Patrick Church in Chatham, I had conducted a Triage for a Donor Bank Drive in the name of a young girl, Carolyn Walsh, who happened to be the niece of my dear friend, Cathy Gilrane. Sweet little Carolyn did ultimately receive a match. However, she lived for only a short while after the transplant. Because of this drive, I was already in the donor bank myself. My sister Susan was a match for me, but since she had had breast cancer and had taken some of the same drugs I had to fight the disease, they did not use her for the match. A thirty-seven-year-old male was a "nine out of ten" match for me, and the doctor selected him. This was the only information I would be given about the donor. If he agreed and I agreed, we could contact each other after a year, but formal papers would have to be signed.

I was due to enter Memorial Sloan Kettering at the end of April. My transplant date would be around May 17, 2004. I would fight to share my new birthday with the memory of my beautiful mother-in-law, Evelyn Grace Koch, and in honor of my niece Tara Hattar, both of whom were born on this same day. I would again be in the hospital for another thirty days followed by one hundred days in isolation at home.

Before I entered the hospital for the transplant, the 9/11 families and team facilitators hosted an incredible luncheon at the home of Pat McNamee, in New Vernon, New Jersey. The families from our 9/11 Group, along with my family, some friends, and Father Paddy were there to send me off. They presented me with an amazing scrapbook of all our days together and another book filled with letters of affirmation from 9/11 families. What a moving day, to say the least. It was difficult and sad for me to say goodbye to all these beautiful people in my life. I was not so sure if I would ever see their heart-warming faces again.

Chapter 29

T cell Transplant: Thirty Days and Born Again

APRIL 2004

A t the end of April 2004, I entered Memorial Sloan Kettering Cancer Center in New York City as planned. All paperwork had been completed and insurance had come through. I had met with a therapist a couple of times beforehand and signed advance directives such as a Living Will and a DNR. The donor's T cells from the bone marrow had arrived. The nurse told me to put on my gown and robe and walk around the quad as much as I could before I entered isolation for thirty days. As I walked up the hallway, I saw a penny on the floor. Whenever I see a stray penny, I pick it up and put it in my pocket. So, I bent down to see if this penny was facing heads up, and, sure enough, it was! This was a good sign, I thought. When I turned the corner, I saw another penny on the floor, not heads up. I picked it up, thinking that there must be a person with a hole in their pocket. When I turned the corner again, there was yet one more penny heads up! On the third side of the quad, there was nothing on the floor. But then I walked back into my room and at the threshold of the doorway was another shiny penny, heads up. I picked up the penny, and what caught my eye were the words, "In God We Trust." I started thinking this was a game the nurse was cajoled into by a small bereavement group I had started before I got ill. One day, some ladies in that group had talked about finding pennies since their spouses' deaths. One gal, Gail, was sure they were pennies from heaven. She seemed to be finding pennies everywhere she went. It was just, too much of a coincidence, she told the group. I was sure her husband, Doug, was now sending pennies to me from above!

In the days ahead, I watched movies and marveled at the scrapbooks given to me by the 9/11 families. Even as early as May, New York City was getting ready to hold the thirty-eighth Republican National Convention, and there were lots of talk shows of what N.Y.C. was doing to accommodate everyone. August 30th thru September 2nd would be a happening time in the Big Apple for sure in this election year as seen on my TV. I walked around in circles to maintain my muscle strength, and I took lots of showers. However, I felt tired, sick, and fatigued from the medicines. I became neutropenic, which means I had a reduction in the number of neutrophils in my blood, a scenario seen in leukemia patients. I was brought down, and then I was ready to receive the new T cells from my donor's bone marrow.

The day came for the transplant. May 17, 2004 became my new birthday. Although I was terribly sick, it just seemed so simple. An injection into my IV of my donor's T cells from his bone marrow, and now I was born again. Everyone around me — doctors and nurses and my daughter Kerry — was saying happy birthday with celebratory voices! Amazing, I thought! If I had felt better, I would have gotten up and danced, but it was not like that. I was living each day, hour, and minute just to stay alive.

On this awesome day of my transplant, my daughter Kerry had made arrangements for a cake to celebrate this special occasion. She had decorated my room at the hospital with curtains and family pictures and a clock adorned with different faces of my granddaughter Grace at every hour. This surely would keep my spirits up. The following morning after the transplant, I got out of bed and listened to, "You Raise Me Up," by Josh Groban. I began journaling a thanksgiving prayer to God and entitled it, "The People of the Wings."

My children, Rob, Jesse, and Kerry, and my husband, Bob, took turns sleeping in a bed across from me each night. They were such good sports, dressed in gowns, gloves, and masks.

I flashed back in my mind to the guided imagery exercise and springboard off of the poem, *In the Garden*, by Susun Weed, which I had used with our 9/11 Group at one of our spring meetings. I had now become the sapling being nurtured back into life and being made strong again. Slowly, each day, just like the families of 9/11, this little sapling began to sprout from the ground, green with dirt standing on its edges all around me. The caring love and prayers showered on me by my family and relatives, by the 9/11 Group, and by neighbors and friends, is what held me up. My cousins, the Lillis sisters, eased my mind when they came to care for Tim. These were the cheerleaders on the sidelines who would contribute to rooting me back into life.

JUNE 2004

I returned home in early June when my numbers leveled out. As my husband drove into the entrance of our property, I saw large colorful posters attached to the trees lining both sides of the driveway. The artwork was creations by the children in our neighborhood to welcome me home. My beautiful and thoughtful neighbors, Dee Wisler and Linda Di Filippo, organized the group, such kind and encouraging people they all are. My daughter Kerry, the nurse, and baby Grace, along with Bunny Neuhart, a dear friend, stood on the front porch dressed in their medical scrubs. Even Grace was in small baby scrubs, holding a sign that read, "MEDICAL TEAM." Tears of euphoria streamed from my eyes, for I did not think I would ever see home again. My sister Noelle came days later from California to live with me for three months. She was a tremendous help. I will always be indebted to her and her family for the time she sacrificed away from them. She brought with her the gift of humor, a gift that gave me hope and helped me to heal.

I was told that I was expected to return with infections maybe two more times. I was also told I needed to stay in a sterile atmosphere for one hundred days. My dog Rudy had to be taken out of our home for that duration of time. I was to be on a neutropenic diet with foods cooked in my home and only cooked fruits and vegetables. The doctors knew what they were saying; I did return to Memorial Sloan Kettering just as they said I would.

One of the dates I returned was September 11, 2004. Since I could not be in attendance at the 9/11 Memorial Mass of Remembrance, I wrote a letter to the group that my daughter Kerry delivered for me. Our group's chairperson and co-chairperson did a wonderful job organizing the day. I do remember that on that day I felt extremely depressed. I started to wonder if I would ever get well again. More so than ever before, I was face-to-face with the reality of my own mortality. From my hospital bed, I watched the ceremonies at Ground Zero. I felt like this was my own Ground Zero day, just a very, very bad day. A few days later, I recovered, and I was released from the hospital. Thanks to the many miracles of Memorial Sloan Kettering Cancer Center and their heroic doctors and nurses.

Chapter 30

Beyond Transplant: With
Thanksgiving in My Heart

DECEMBER 2004

T ime went by slowly. Christmas was coming, and I did my shopping online and through catalogs. One day at my front door, I found a large black bag filled with beautifully wrapped Christmas gifts tied up with satin ribbons of red, white, blue, and green. Attached to these little treasures were letters and holiday cards from the 9/11 families, most with family photos. The best gifts were the cards and the smiles on the faces of the family members.

As I opened the gifts, I was astonished to see that many of them were angel ornaments for our tree. I flashed back to the prayer Annie Greenleaf had written for our group. Her words echoed in my mind, "When you think that there is an angel around you, know that there are thousands." I guessed they just wanted these celestial beings to watch over me, and that they did!

One evening, the week before Christmas, friends from Chatham appeared at my front door. It was such a delight to see these familiar jolly faces, bundled in red and white Santa hats. They sang, "We Wish You a Merry Christmas, and Silent Night," among other carols. These wise friends brought the true Spirit of the Epiphany on this dark and chilly eve as stars shown brightly in the sky, they placed me right at the Manger and touched my heart with the gift of joy.

After the carolers left, I flashed back to the many Christmas' in years past when I had coordinated the Ministry to the Sick at Saint Patrick Church in Chatham, N.J. One of my favorite events to organize was our Saint Patrick Church Youth Group caroling event. We would visit our sick and homebound parishioners around Chatham, singing Christmas carols to them. I could still remember the delight on the people's faces. Our visits would warm their hearts as their expressions lit up with delight. I had come full circle on this oh, so festive and significant eve as we drew close to the Christ Child's birth.

MARCH 30, 2004

I had moved past my one hundred days of isolation, and I was getting stronger and functioning well. I received a phone call one day from our group chairperson. Jeanne told me, I had been invited by New Jersey Governor James McGreevey and Commissioner Susan Bass Levin, to the Governor's Mansion in Princeton, New Jersey in celebration of 2004 Women's History Month. At the event, I would receive the *Wynona M. Lipman and Connie Woodruff Award*. I was shocked, to say the least!

My doctor gave me permission to attend the ceremony. Unfortunately, my husband would be away on business at this time. My dear friend Jim McNamee kindly offered to pick me up and escort me to the Governor's Mansion at Drumthwacket. I had no idea that I would be riding in a limousine. I felt like Cinderella! I was sure that on that night I was in a fairy tale! Several members of our group were also with me. I felt so honored. What a grand night, I thought, when the night came to an end. Not only did it boost my spirits, but also my immune system as well!

Months later I was contacted by *the Cancer Hope Network* to receive yet another award, and on May 17, 2004, (my AML birthday) I, also received *The Saint Angela Award* from the Ursuline School in

New Rochelle, New York. These turns of events were just all incredibly overwhelming and unbelievable to me.

Almost fifteen years have now passed since the nightmare of my journey through AML leukemia. I have met six new grandchildren who have given me so much delight, and a deep sense of renewal. I am most thankful to the many people who supported our family throughout these difficult days. You gave me hope; you brought me back into life.

I wrote a prayer the morning after the transplant thinking of all of those who reached out to us:

A PRAYER OF THANKSGIVING AMONG THE WINGS

Oh, Great Creator of wondrous acts of love
Of all those people who are wise and awesome
Thank you for the people of the wings who raise us up
When times are trying.
Thank you for the risk takers for life
Most especially Michael Clark who said, "Yes"
That a stranger might know life
Thank you for the peacemakers and the healers,
Our family and friends, nurses, doctors, and caregivers
Of
Every kind.
They are the shadow of you in our midst.
Bountiful, bless them all for their goodness and light.
Continue to send them like butterflies over the gardens of life
That they might multiply
And hold up others in the darkness by their wings to behold their beauty.

Written with Love,
Pam Koch

Transformative Grief in Action

The most beautiful people we have known are those who have known defeat. Known Suffering. Known struggle. Known loss. And have found their way out of the depths. These persons have an appreciation, a sensitivity, and an understanding of life that fills them with compassion, gentleness, and a deep loving concern. Beautiful people do not just happen.

Elizabeth Kubler-Ross

On the following pages, I am pleased and honored to present several of The Saint James 9/11 Bereavement Support Group families who will share the actions they have taken to keep alive the memory of their deceased loved ones.

It was not only those included in this book, but also all the other group members who have extended countless good works to others too numerous to mention. They all came into my life after the disaster of 9/11 and they all were beautiful people. I watched them suffer and struggle to know loss in such a raw way. All the while it was the beauty of their hearts I was focusing on. They became close to one another and helped to heal one another.

These following inspiring stories illustrate the power of transformative grief. Through the dark times, these families followed their faith in God and in themselves. They made hard choices. They took risks. They were courageous, resilient, and patient. They persevered, and they endured until they found their way back into their journey of life. They found creative ways to amplify the goodness of their lost loved ones, birthing their names back into the world in another way and making it a better place in which to live.

MICHAEL P. O'BRIEN

In the years since The Saint James 9/11 Bereavement Support Group, much has happened in the O'Brien family. In 2006 I heard about an organization that helps grieving children. I became a volunteer at "Good Grief". Their mission is to support grieving children and their families so no child grieves alone. In 2008 I became a group facilitator and facilitated children's groups from the age of three to eighteen. In 2010 I joined the staff of "Good Grief" as their Program Coordinator. "Good Grief" has grown tremendously over the years. We now have a center in Princeton, New Jersey, as well as in Morristown, New Jersey. We acquired our own home in Princeton. The dedication and ribbon cutting was held on September 19, 2015. One of the rooms in the home will be named *The Michael P. O'Brien Orientation Room*. This is the room where the grieving families first learn about the services that "Good Grief" offers.

My daughter, Sarah, has graduated with her masters in School Counseling. She is now taking classes to specialize in grief and loss. It is her passion to support grieving children just as she was supported. My youngest son Kevin is a senior at Quinnipiac University. He is majoring in Game Design and Development. At his internship this summer, he is working on creating a video game to help grieving children navigate their "new normal."

There are two scholarships in Mike's name. One is *The Michael P. O'Brien Memorial Fund* at New Hartford High School in New Hartford,

New York. Mike graduated from there in 1977. This is awarded to a senior who most resembles the qualities that Mike possessed — hardworking, caring, and community minded. The second scholarship was given at the college where Mike and I graduated from, SUNY Oswego in Oswego, New York. This was a scholarship created by Mike's roommate.

We remember and honor Mike every day. Thank you for letting the world know about the people who touched our lives and continue to touch others.

Mike made everyone feel happy.

He lived without hesitation.

He danced like no one was watching.

He lived in the moment and made the moments memorable.

He was a peacemaker.

He was a great golfer and honored the game with his talent and grace.

He loved his family.

Mike honored the gift of life and he shared his love of life with everyone he met.

A note from Pam: *The O'Brien family has taken their grief to another level you made the choice to go to a higher plateau to help others wounded in grief. May you abundantly be blessed, each of you, for reaching out to the bereaved. You have readjusted and adapted new ways of being in this world aiding the bereaved.*

DAVID O. CAMPBELL

Dave was a senior vice president at Keefe Bruyette & Woods. He died on 9/11 at the age of fifty-one in his office in the South Tower of the World Trade Center.

The David O. Campbell Memorial Scholarship was formed at Delbarton School in Randolph, New Jersey. *The David O. Campbell Ice Hockey Locker Room* was named by Delbarton School.

Delbarton was where Dave was so very proud to have his sons, Chip and Timmy, attend school. Dave thought so highly of the school. We all continue to support it, and that bond continues.

With our Basking Ridge friends, we celebrate Dave with an annual Paddle Tennis Tournament. As a family, we are private in the grief and healing process. We are very close with each other and talk about Dave a lot. Cindy helps with the planning of the 9/11 Memorial Mass of Remembrance each anniversary; she is the treasurer for this special time.

A Note from Pam: *Dave was Cindy's friend during high school, but he became her sweetheart in college. Dave was a dedicated father to Chip and Timmy and was known as successful and fun loving.*

Chip, Dave's son, writes in a college essay, "I will carry the effects of September 11th with me every day for the rest of my life: I write of it's importance to me with the understanding that such writing is a vital part of the healing process. As a result of your careful guidance and teaching, I feel completely confident in the way you and mom have brought me up and will carry the values you have instilled in me for the rest of my life."

Dave taught this young man and his brother everything a loving and wise father could ever give to his sons: a life lived richly in morals, principals, values, and in faith. I have no doubt Chip, as well as Timmy, will be as successful as their devoted father was in life, as they carry these essential attributes with them to make this world a better place in Dave's name. Transformative actions at their best!

ROBERT J. HALLIGAN

A fund is in the process of being created by Robert's wife, Jerrie Halligan. Jerrie writes, "Robert had dyslexia, and he was an extremely talented musician. Robert was born in England, so I want the trust fund to honor the British Dyslexia Association for dyslexic children who demonstrate potential with their musical talents. I met Robert in Paris, France, at the Concorde Lafayette Hotel when I walked into the hotel elevator. One year later, we were married. We lived an "English love storybook life" until the attacks on the WTC. At the time of 9/11, I became part of The Saint James 9/11 Bereavement Support Group. When this group was all together, I felt empowerment. It was inspiring, you want to go on and help others."

A Note from Pam: *It was so nice, Jerrie, having you in our group. You were a gift to us all. Spread Roberts love wherever you travel!*

JOHN W. FARRELL

Maryanne Farrell was a member of The Saint James 9/11 Bereavement Support Group from its very beginning. Her husband, John, was killed while working at Sandler O'Neill Inc. in the South Tower on September 11, 2001.

In 2004 Maryanne's sister, Megan McDowell, a social worker who lived at Maryanne's house for six weeks after the terrorist attacks, created a non-profit organization in their hometown of Basking Ridge in daily memory of her brother-in-law, John. "Heartworks" is a 501(C3) Acts of Kindness group that replicates the type of kindness people showed her sister and her four children in the weeks and months after 9/11.

The "Heartworks" philosophy represents the combination of ideas and sentiments Megan witnessed from volunteering for 9/11 support groups, as well as individual gestures that the community offered her sister's family. This organization offers an opportunity for women and families to show kindness to people experiencing illness, grief, and unexpected tragedy. They host monthly meetings for over seventy women and focus on prayer, organizing for families in need of hope, and inspirational messages that focus on gratitude, receiving, and giving. "Heartworks" has an email list of over six hundred women wanting to continue the kindness that began on 9/11. They have assisted hundreds of families and given away well over a million dollars in the past ten years. Every day "Heartworks" volunteers are reaching out to people experiencing illness and loss by delivering meals and gifts; offering pet walking, food shopping, holiday decorating, and rides to appointments; dropping off fun surprises; providing needed vacations and nights out; funding music lessons, camps, and other activities for children; and so much more! Maryanne is an active member of "Heartworks" and spends much of her time paying forward what was offered to her family in 2001.

Maryanne helps in forming the Offertory Procession for the Memorial Mass each anniversary. Candles from this day are taken to others experiencing grief from the families of 9/11 Anniversary Memorial each year.

A Note from Pam: *Way to go, girls! You have made a difference in our world in a big way! Your positive expression of love for those who are in need and hurting is inspiring. If every town had a "Heartworks" what a wonderful world this would be! This family has certainly reinvested emotional energy into new people in your lives in an outstanding way.*

THOMAS PATRICK KNOX

Thomas Patrick Knox, or Tommy as his family and friends called him, was the youngest son of six children, born to Pat and Harry Knox on November 22, 1969. He was an adored younger brother to Jim, Denis, Mary Ellen, Patty, and Kathleen.

He married the love of his life, Nancy, on October 6, 2000. Tremendous fun and happy times were had by all that day! He was an energy broker at Cantor Fitzgerald and thirty-one years old at the time of his death. Tommy is survived by his mother Pat, and his wife Nancy, and with five siblings, also ten nephews and nieces, and with many extended family and friends. His funeral mass had over 2,000 people in attendance, and at the repast afterward, there were probably as many at his mother's and sister's house in Basking Ridge.

Nancy, mom, and I attended a support group at Saint James. I would urge my other sisters to attend, but they needed to work and could not spend the time. Whatever we worked on or the special activities we experienced, we would share with my family afterward. Little did we know we learned skills on how to get up every day and live, despite all the pain we were feeling.

The Thomas Patrick Knox Memorial Scholarship at Seton Hall Prep in West Orange, New Jersey, was founded in 2002. To date the scholarship has provided yearly scholarships to twenty-one deserving students, totaling $128,000. The first event was held at The Liberty House Restaurant in Jersey City. This restaurant overlooks the Hudson Bay, with a view of downtown Manhattan and also Ground Zero, which is now the Freedom Tower site. Each year the scholarship recipients would attend our function, and a video dedication of Tommy's life would air, in essence introducing each student to Tommy and the Knox family.

> *The Thomas P. Knox Memorial Foundation* was founded in 2004.
> Consisting of the Executive Board of directors:
> President, Nancy Knox, Tom's wife,
> Vice President, Kathleen Knox Doolan, Tom's sister
> Secretary/Treasurer, Patricia Knox Lalley, Tom's sister
>
> Other Board Members include:
> Denis Knox
> Jim Knox
> Mary Ellen Knox
> *As well as six other family members and friends of Tommy's

We hold our annual meeting at the Doolans' house every 9/11 after we attend the Memorial Mass of Remembrance.

Tommy's nieces and nephews also help in fundraising, as well as administrative duties, and projects to ship care packages to our soldiers.

Other fundraising events include the *Annual McGovern's Tavern Golf Outing* held every June for the past thirteen years. Tommy's buddies, in particular Patrick McGovern, as well as former classmates, teammates, friends, and family, gather together to play golf and then return to McGovern's Tavern in Newark to reminisce and share some laughs.

In 2016, we held an event at Liberty House to commemorate the fifteenth anniversary. This event went from yearly to bi-annually and now on special anniversaries.

Unfortunately, there were several natural disasters that occurred after 9/11. The tsunami of 2004, Hurricane Katrina in 2005, and the earthquake in Haiti in 2010, just to name a few. *The Thomas P. Knox Foundation* was able to make memorial donations in Tommy's name to the charities set up to help children after these horrific natural disasters.

The Thomas P. Knox Foundation is committed to honoring our veterans through donations to *The Fisher House Foundation*, which is best known for a network of comfort homes where military and veterans' families can stay at no cost while a loved one is receiving treatment.

The Thomas Knox Foundation, in keeping with the support of our troops, also has made donations in Tommy's name to the *Adopt a Soldier Program*. Also, aid has been given to *The Intrepid Fallen Soldiers Fund*, which has provided close to $150 million in support for the families of military personnel lost in service to our nation, and to severely, wounded military personnel and veterans.

Since cancer has touched the lives of *The Thomas P. Knox Foundation* members, donations have been made to *The Leukemia and Lymphoma Society*, and also to *The Lustgarten Foundation*.

The Thomas P. Knox Foundation has also supported "Heartworks", an Acts of Kindness group founded by Megan McDowell, whose brother-in-law, John Farrell, also perished on this horrific day. *The Thomas P. Knox Foundation* has contributed to *Camp Better Days*, an outreach for children of 9/11 founded by Amy Callahan.

In all, since its inception, the Foundation has donated more than $224,000 to help others while remembering our Tommy. It is a labor of love that we continue to operate this day. The family is committed to honoring Tommy always, helping others in need, and making this world a better place as we continue on our grief journey here on earth.

Unfortunately, we are sad to share, two bright and talented Seton Hall Prep graduates who were the recipients of *The Thomas P. Knox Scholarship* died at the age of nineteen. Michael McCormick Jr. died in a car accident in August 2009. Then Brendan Tevlin died June 25, 2014. Brendan was murdered by a self-proclaimed jihadist just up the street from Seton Hall Prep in West Orange. Much like the horror of 9/11, he was taken too soon because of hate and evil. His parents and family stood by our side as we mourned our Tommy and as we held events every year. Now we all stand by them in their hour of need, as we do also with Michael McCormick's family. Both of these families have started foundations and scholarships in memory of their dearly cherished sons gone way too soon. Both of these young men, Michael McCormick and Brendan Tevlin, were beacons of light and deeply loved by their families. All who knew and loved them will sorely miss them.

- *The Michael T. McCormick Jr. Scholarship* at Seton Hall Prep
- *The* Michael T. McCormick Jr. Scholarship at Penn State University
- *The Brendan Patrick Tevlin Memorial Fund* Seton Hall Prep
- The re-naming of the Athletic Field at Seton Hall Prep in Brendan Tevlin's name.

In March 2013 Billy Zimmerman, a friend of my oldest son, Jack, was tragically killed in a car accident. Jack took it upon himself, with support of many friends and classmates, to organize a basketball classic to gather the family and friends of his dear friend, Billy, while raising money for his scholarship at Seton Hall Prep. Jack was only eight years old when 9/11 occurred, and it had a lasting effect on all the children in our family. Jack was nineteen when his friend died, and having seen how our family healed as we all grieved after 9/11, he used the tools he learned as a young boy to make something positive come out of something so senseless and painful. All the Knox nephews and nieces learned that valuable lesson from an early age.

The Saint James 9/11 Bereavement Support Group for our 9/11 families gave my family the tools to enable us to transform our grief into action. In doing so, we are now able to help those who have experienced traumatic grief and pay forward what was given to us.

A Note from Pam: *Kathleen Doolan helped to coordinate the 9/11 Memorial Mass of Remembrance for many years at the Shrine of Saint Joseph in Stirling, New Jersey. Kathleen received "The Tree Of Life Award" for her constant effort to keep us connected, informed, and acted on our behalf many times. We will be forever grateful to you Kathleen for your time and energy. It was my pleasure to work with you. Your transformative grief in action is commendable.*

KEVIN J. HANNAFORD SR

The Kevin Hannaford Foundation created by his wife, Eileen A. Hannaford, who is President and Executive Director. Sons Kevin and Patrick Hannaford help Eileen much of the time.

The Kevin J. Hannaford, Sr. Foundation, Inc. was named for Kevin J. Hannaford, Sr., who was killed in the September 11, 2001 terrorist attacks on the World Trade Center in New York. We are keeping Kevin's memory alive and helping our community by continuing to assist local children, who suffered the loss of a parent, in pursuing educational and enrichment opportunities. It is our hope, through our gifts, each child will feel loved and supported and develop into healthy, giving adults.

Here are some of the accomplishments of the Foundation. Over the past eleven years, over ninety gifts have been made to academic and enrichment programs on behalf of the children who have lost parents in the Basking Ridge and Bernardsville, New Jersey, area. The recipients range in age from pre-school to college. Along with individual scholarships, we have given gifts to the following organizations that support our mission:

- *The Better Days Foundation*
- Catholic Charities
- Coalition of 911 Families
- Seton Hall Preparatory
- *Somerset Hills YMCA Strong Kids Program*
- *Tuesday's Children*
- *UNICEF*

A Note from Pam: *Eileen still makes time to aid others in any way she can, through the foundation named for her husband. The Coalition of 9/11 Families runs many events including a Family Fun Day, Christmas Tree Sale, Swim-a-thon, and a Vineyard Vines Sales Day at the retailer's store in the Short Hills mall. At the Vineyard Vines Sales Day held in December 2014, twenty percent of the proceeds were generously donated to The Brendan Patrick Tevlin Memorial Fund at Seton Hall Preparatory School. Eileen donates her time in helping to create the Memorial Mass of Remembrance. The motto for The Kevin J. Hannaford, Sr. Foundation is "Together we can make a difference, one child at a time." And you have, Eileen, many times over in Kevin's name. So very proud to know this woman of excellence and watching her boys follow in her footsteps.*

MICHAEL B. FINNEGAN

The Michael B. Finnegan Foundation, Inc.
(Can be found on Facebook)

Erin, Mike's wife, writes, "We formed *The Michael B. Finnegan Golf Classic* with proceeds donated to the Juvenile Diabetes Research Foundation and *the Make-A-Wish Foundation*. We then founded a golf school in Florida, which is *The Michael B. Finnegan Learning Center* at the *First Tee of the Palm Beaches*. I am on this board and have been since they founded it. Now I'm on an honorary board with Jack Nicklaus because we were able to open two more golf schools in Florida to help physically and mentally challenged children, as well as underprivileged and mainstream kids. They learn life lessons through the game of golf. We have a curriculum the kids must pass about healthy habits and values before they can play golf. It is really fantastic! My daughter, Bridget worked there as an instructor last summer."

A Note from Pam: *Erin also did volunteer work for a concert given in the memory of Brendan Tevlin, the young man who was killed in a terrorist attack in West Orange, New Jersey. He was a Seton Hall graduate.*

Michael's love for the game of golf carries on through the children who have been blessed by his name. Erin your transformative grief reaction is amazing! Erin is a joy to know and was a bright spirit in our group.

LOUIS V. FERSINI JR.

Cathy Fersini writes – After raising my children alone, Chris turning nine on September 13, 2001, the twins being two, and Brian was only seven when Louis died; I truly thought I would be alone forever. I dated, had fun with the amazing girls in the group, but fun was all it was. I stayed home with my children. I then met an amazing man. It was a time in my life when I resigned myself to thinking that just staying home with my kids was good. We met at his bakery, which is located right near my parents' home and where my sister worked in her teenage years. He also has four kids like me; only he has three girls and a boy. I have three boys and a girl. We took our time. Life is good. The kids absolutely love each other. They all respect us and enjoy us being their parents. It is not to say that my kids don't wish every day that their dad was here for them. I still love my Louis and will never forget him and the life we had together. I am sad to hear people say, 'Oh, she's re-married and happy, and 9/11 is behind her.' It's never behind me. It is never behind my children and my family. We may have moved forward, but we can never forget. I am blessed for a second time, but

I will never forget. Every year's anniversary of 9/11, I am thankful for the healing our Saint James 9/11 Bereavement Support Group gave to me, and the ability to transfer that healing onto my children. The mother/ step mother of eight!"

A Note from Pam: *Cathy was also busy at the time of Hurricane Sandy. Through the efforts of her family bakery, she made hundreds of sandwiches and baked goods each day to distribute to the people devastated by the storm that left many homeless. She worked tirelessly in aiding people for many days.*

Cathy is the mother of two boys who attended Seton Hall Preparatory School. She never stops giving. At the time of Brendan Tevlin's shooting in West Orange, New Jersey, she supported efforts to aid the family and also Brendan's fund through the school. Cathy also is on the team for the Memorial Mass of Remembrance on the 9/11 Anniversary each year as a lector. We are most grateful for her outreach and love through her transformative grief in action. Most certainly Louis will never be forgotten for his name lives on in Cathy's goodness and love to others.

THOMAS BARNES REINIG

Jeanne Fattori Reinig Smith:

Tom had just started a new position at e-Speed on the 105th floor of the North Tower when 9/11 occurred. After many long months of grieving, my brain started to function again. We need to smile and to laugh and to remember the wonderful times we had with our loved ones. They wouldn't want us to be hurting so much. As my son says, "Don't cry because it is over; smile because it happened." Let us continue to celebrate all their lives – be happy again. I am trying my best because Tom would have expected this from me. If I can do it, so can you.

Jeanne and her boys, Scott and Chris, put transformative grief in action as follows:

- *The Thomas Barnes Reinig Academic Scholarship* at Delbarton School.
- *The Thomas Barnes Reinig and Jeanne Fattori Reinig Smith Scholarship* at Cornell University.

A Note from Pam: *Tom's wife, Jeanne, was the first chairperson of our Saint James 9/11 Bereavement Support Group. Jeanne used her time wisely and helped to coordinate the third year Anniversary Mass of Remembrance at the Shrine of Saint Joseph in Stirling, New Jersey. She creatively worked in the basement of her home on a scrapbook with the story of our group in picture form. Jeanne, along with Elise Krevis and Betsy Schulenburg, joined together on the project.*

Jeanne believes in paying it forward. What really got her through her very hard days was her volunteering. She was an avid volunteer teaching gymnastics to special needs children at our YMCA and also teaching swimming for the Special Olympics going forward after 9/11. Jeanne's outreach continued with hospital volunteer work after moving to Naples, Florida. Her outreach to others has been notable. She, along with her co-chairperson, Susan Picarro, continued on with the group after I became ill. They performed an exemplary job! They are both heroes in my eyes!

F. PAUL WISNIEWSKI

Carol, Allie, and Jonathan

Paul deeply loved his family, especially his children, Allie and Jonathan. We belonged to the Liberty Corner Presbyterian Church in Basking Ridge at the time of his call to heaven. I wanted to honor his memory so we could remember Paul in a lovely light and also meet a need of our church. After consideration and conversing with Steve McConnell, who was the pastor of our church at that time, we decided the way to honor God and remember Paul was to build a playground in his memory.

The inscription on the granite stone reads **as follows:**

THIS PLAYGROUND IS DEDICATED
IN LOVING MEMORY OF
F. PAUL WISNIEWSKI
FEBRUARY 10, 1947–SEPTEMBER 11, 2001

(Matt. 19:14)
Jesus said, "Let the children come to me
And do not hinder them, for the kingdom
Of heaven belongs to such as these."

~

Gray silver this day
Gray silver his hair
Gray silver his car
Gray silver his glasses
Gray silver the ferry
Gray silver the tower
Gray silver the airplane
Gray silver the ash
Gray silver the reflection of the candle wax in the court
Gray silver the hymnal
Gray silver the three doves, one going home
Gray silver cobblestone where we met
Gray silver the seven pools
Gray silver the color of our house
Gray silver the ladder he used to climb
Gray silver the path to our front door
Gray silver our cat Monet
Gray silver our beach chairs
Gray silver his watch from Vietnam
Gray silver his jacket

Gray silver his tie
Gray silver his mustache
Gray silver his favorite sweatshirt
Gray silver the shirt he wore last
Gray silver the mirror
Gray silver the reflection of a man whose
soul was so very kind and gentle
Gray silver the lining of the clouds that reflect
down upon us from heaven
Gray silver our memories

In our hearts with love until we meet again,
Carol, Allie, and Jonathan

A Note from Pam: *Sterling silver is the memory of you, Carol, for so many in our group. Your family's, transformative grief in action project, will put smiles on many children's faces while keeping Paul's name alive for many years into the future.*

MATTHEW C. SELLITTO

Loreen Sellitto, mother of Matthew, 23, North Tower, 105th Floor:

The first time I left my house after the attacks, I wasn't prepared to see all the signs everywhere in support of our country and in tribute to the victims. I could see American flags all along the roads, in peoples' yards, and on their homes; and all the signs of support — UNITED WE STAND, YOU ARE NOT ALONE, GOD BLESS THE 9/11 VICTIMS AND FAMILIES.

I realized that this was going to be a very public loss for me; I was more than a mother grieving the death of her son. I was also an American whose country had been attacked, and I wanted to find a way to make a difference.

My husband, Matt, and I joined several groups going to Washington, DC, to lobby for the *9/11 Commission* and later worked as members of *the Family Steering Committee* once the Commission was established.

I am so very proud of *the Matthew C. Sellitto Foundation* started in 2002. We have awarded over eighty academic scholarships, established endowment programs in three institutions of higher learning, and support educational training workshops on 9/11-based curricula. Various family members volunteer at *the 9/11 Tribute Center*, NYC, by giving tours of the memorial to the general public.

9/11 forced my family to find a "new normal" in our lives. Our work in Washington and the *MCS Foundation* helped to create an environment of healing for us.

A Note from Pam: Matt and Loreen have been outstanding voices of hope on behalf of the 9/11 families, keeping Matthew's memory alive. Many days they both spent lobbying in Washington, DC, and giving talks with senators and congressmen as well governors seeking to get laws passed. They have been successful in their quest. Both Matt and Loreen also have volunteered as docents at the Memorial at Ground Zero.

It is with a heavy, saddened heart that I learned Matt and Loreen's second and only other child, Jonathan, died suddenly at the age of thirty-four. He leaves a wife and three-year-old daughter. Until we meet again may God hold you, Jonathan and Matthew tenderly close to His heart.

LUDWIG J. PICARRO

"He was a great guy." Ludwig Picarro, born in New Castle, Pennsylvania, was forty-four years old at the time of the attack on the World Trade Center. Lud, as he was sometimes called, was a senior vice president for the insurance company, Zurich U.S., for seventeen years at the time of 9/11. His office was across the street from the World Trade Center. On 9/11 he was at a meeting on the 104th floor of the South Tower of the World Trade Center. He was a devoted husband and a family man including a big fan of his two boys and their sports activities.

A Note from Pam: *Susan Picarro, wife of Ludwig, gave so much of her time after 9/11 when our group decided to go forward. She continued to help others wounded in grief, going for Bereavement Training in the Metuchen Diocese of New Jersey, and then starting a bereavement group at Saint James Church. As co-chairperson of our Saint James 9/11 Bereavement Support Group and then chairperson, Susan was also instrumental in keeping our group connected with the plan that we had devised earlier. For several years, she helped to coordinate the Memorial Mass of Remembrance and often hosted brunches around the event at her warm and lovely home. She was also a gracious hostess at Christmas time, gathering our Saint James 9/11 Bereavement Support Group together. Susan later became the chairperson when Jeanne Reinig stepped down. Susan aided my own family during my illness, and I can never forget her goodness all of the way. I miss her and think about her often. She ultimately moved and relocated to a warmer climate.*

KAREN L. SEYMOUR

Karen was the loving wife of William Dietrich and mother of three-year-old twins, William and Sarah, when 9/11 happened. She was attending a seminar on the 106th floor when the plane hit. She was a talented Wall Street technology specialist, an excellent cook, and an avid cyclist.

The Karen L. Seymour Memorial Fund was established at Liberty Science Center, Jersey City, New Jersey. This fund's goal was to encourage greater global harmony by educating children and families of all backgrounds in the peaceful use of science and technology. Almost any useful purpose can be tied to aid the tragedy on September 11, 2001.

Never shall I forget that day, the day in September, which has changed my life so drastically.

Never shall I forget the faces on my little children when I told them of their mother's death.

Never shall I forget the images of such devastation that took my beautiful, young wife's life away from me, and challenged my faith and perspective of the world forever.

Bill encouraged the group to be influential in making changes to prevent similar tragedies from happening again. Several members of our group are working in that direction and will continue to do so in the years ahead.

A Note from Pam: *Bill is a courageous and brave father who has brought up his twins with love and support. He has done an incredible job. Bill was committed to his grief work, and he was a delight to have in the group!*

TIMOTHY SOULAS

Katy Soulas, spouse

I am deeply touched that Pam, or Pammielamb as we affectionately call her, has asked me to tell a little bit of my story. On September 11, 2001, I was eleven weeks pregnant with our sixth child when my husband, Tim, became a victim of the terrorist attacks, leaving me alone to raise our sons, then eleven, nine, seven, and five years old, and our daughter, nineteen months of age. I was blessed to be surrounded by my and Tim's amazing families, countless friends, wonderful neighbors, a giving community, and a nation that opened its hearts to all of us closely affected by the disaster.

My faith in God is what allowed me to get through those endlessly tearful, heartbreaking days and months. I had worked as an Emergency Department nurse since college graduation and was more than familiar with sudden death and families' reactions. On 9/11, I knew it was my turn to survive this ordeal, to nurture my children, and to create a loving home. My faith was challenged: I had to accept that God's plan was quite different than mine and Tim's and that He would give me the strength and the courage to meet the obstacles ahead.

On that dreadful night, my home was bursting with family and friends from our hometown, a suburb of Philadelphia, with thirty-two people bunking on couches, in my kids' beds, and on neighbors' inflatable mattresses. My five children were in my bed, restless, hoping daddy would walk in the door. To settle them I began to say the rosary, a litany of prayers to the mother of Jesus, a mantra to lull my excited and agitated children to rest. The children fell peacefully to sleep, and I caressed my slightly swollen pregnant tummy. I then experienced the most profound moment of my life. I felt God's presence; His peace embraced me with warmth. Our bedroom was glowing, and I knew Tim was safe in God's heavenly kingdom. I knew he did not want me to wonder how he suffered, because it did not matter now. I felt a serenity that my children, my unborn baby, and I were going to be OK. I did not sleep that night, or for many nights since then, but that moment of peace will be with me forever.

We were touched by love and service by thousands of people in ways I can barely list. My favorites were handmade cards from children all over the world that encouraged my kids, homework help, a cleaning service, a pile of necessities like toilet paper, lunch box treats, and drinks left in my driveway, a donation of $11 from a boy who sold apples on his corner, and friends and coaches who made sure our sons had rides to football and ice hockey practices! I believe all of these acts of generosity and kindness came straight from God, and those people were my angels to boost my children and me into our, "new normal."

Despite being surrounded by love, I was internally dark. Anxiety of the future plagued me, and depression was heavy. I learned that my children are the greatest teachers and spiritual guides! Just before Halloween in 2001, I brought all five children to a local farm to hike, ride in a hay wagon, make our way through a corn maze, eat donuts and cider, and pick apples. The boys only wanted the apples from the top of the tree and had to use a crazy contraption to do so. I was wistfully watching moms and dads with their children, whole families. But my sons were belly-laughing as the apples would fall and one or the other would dive for the catch. My nine-year-old looked at me with a silly grin and said, "Mom, is this the first time since Dad died that we are all laughing and having fun again?" It was a breakthrough for me!

My children taught me that they could feel the grief and pain of Daddy's death, but discovered that they can be happy simultaneously! My feelings of loss and depression led me to the discovery that the pain that caused it was allowing my children and me a deeper appreciation for simple moments of joy. My family, which I mistakenly viewed as broken since Tim's death, was succeeding not despite our wounds, but because of them.

I was ignited with a new determination that God wanted something good to come from all of this. I was voted to be the spokesperson for The Saint James 9/11 Bereavement Support Group. At times, with their input, I wrote speeches and delivered them at Rutgers University in front of the governor and the senators from the state of New Jersey. I continued to represent our families of 9/11, speaking at town hall events filled with agencies, such as the FBI, FEMA, the American Red Cross, and other top governmental agencies. I addressed many groups, as well as over eight hundred families of 9/11 victims. I spoke about what we families needed in terms of support: a 9/11 investigative committee to find out how the event of 9/11 happened and thus to prevent another attack on our country ever again; good health care for our families; not deporting family members whose spouse had a green card and children who were born citizens, yet they were not; the *Tax Relief Bill*; and, finally, *the Victims Compensation Fund*, so families did not have to sue airlines.

I delivered speeches at our local town memorials and the dedication at the bell tower, as well as at our anniversary Memorial Mass of Remembrance. During the memorials, I told the story of my family and my Tim. I told of the grief that we all felt because of the devastating event of 9/11 and the faith that was holding us up. This was the beginning of my journey of public speaking. I was invited twice by Senator Jon Corzine to attend the *State of the Union Address*. I attended the first one, at which President George W. Bush addressed the nation. Several times I went back to Washington, D.C., to give a talk and then lobbied on the Green in front of the Capitol Building for the creation of the 9/11 Commission.

I have been blessed to speak to students and families about faith and hope in times of fear and turmoil. Meditation and journaling have become a part of my healing, and I teach that, too.

I have learned not to underestimate the power of action. A small gesture, a touch, a smile, a kind word, a listening ear can change a person's day, for better or for worse. I know God puts us all in each other's lives to make an impact. God gave us our ability to bond with each other for strength to transcend grief and adversity. God wants us to forgive others, like the terrorists, and those who wrong us, and ourselves, because we were not created to be perfect. We humans have a remarkable power to endure, with faith, hope, and love!

A Note from Pam: *Well said, Katy! Your journey has been one of much pain and suffering, but your perseverance and centering on the God of all hopefulness will prevail. Tim is with you all of the time, just in another way.*

THOMAS STRADA

My Grief Story, written by Terry Strada

My grief has been a long, hard, and complex process that continues to this day. By telling my story, I hope in some small way to help you with your grief or whatever journey you may be on. A sudden, premature, horrific loss of someone you love is unlike anything you have ever experienced and something you can never prepare for.

I'm sure the question you want answered is "How did I get through it?" Sadly, there is no quick fix or easy way to travel the path of grief. It takes hard work, determination, and time. I am fourteen years into my loss, and I have never been able to get all the way through my grief.

When my husband Tom was murdered, I lost my forever partner whom I loved with all my heart and soul. Tom loved me with every fiber of his being and loved our three children more than life itself. He was a devoted family man, loved deeply by his children, parents, siblings, and extended family and friends. He was an avid outdoorsman, scratch golfer, and the most charismatic man I have ever known. He had a successful career on Wall Street as a corporate bond broker and was a partner at his firm, something he was very proud of. But his most treasured pride and joy was his children, and he is deeply missed by all of us. His murder at the hands of hate-filled terrorists was a terrifying experience. Fear and pain crept into my heart and became a part of me. It crept into my children's hearts as well, and I had to put my suffering aside in order to help them with their grief process as best I could.

Grief physically hurts, it can be paralyzing, and it is greedy. It slithered into every second of every minute of every hour of every day crippling me at times with fear, anguish, and pain. Then it would follow me into the night, never allowing for sleep or rest. Grief swallows you, and it changes you.

My grief journey began on September 11, 2001. I don't know when or if it will ever end, but it no longer has the hold on me it once had. In the aftermath of the death and destruction of the worst terrorist attack on American soil, not only was my husband, and father of my children gone, but also numerous friends and colleagues were gone. If I didn't have three young children to take care of, I easily could have attended over twenty-five funerals and memorials of people I once knew and shared a life with.

To complicate matters, Tom was not just murdered; he was also missing. And to this day, we have never received any recovery of his remains. His unidentified body parts, along with over one thousand other victims, are currently housed at the 9/11 National Memorial in New York City. As advances in science are made, new identifications are still happening each year.

As time went on, wallowing in my broken heart and lost dreams and drowning in my sadness was something I could either continue to allow to rule my life, or I could change the course of my destiny and try to find happiness again. I knew I needed to be strong for my children and try and set a good example. The saying "What doesn't kill you makes you stronger" made me angry. I am not stronger because terrorists murdered my husband. I am strong because I had strong loving parents who set good examples, and I wanted to give my children the best examples possible.

From the very beginning, I was angry. My children were seven years old, four years old, and four days old. My country had been attacked on 9/11 by radical Islamic terrorists, and friends had been murdered, my husband was dead, and my children were fatherless. I became a widow at the age of thirty-eight when my marriage ended abruptly and cruelly on 9/11.

I became obsessed with the "who, what, and why" such a devastating terrorist attack on American soil could take place. The more I learned about the attacks, the angrier I became, and the more I wanted answers. I became one of thousands of victims' family members to file a lawsuit against those who gave financial and logistical support to the nineteen hijackers and their plotters. I believed then, and I still do, that utilizing our civil justice system would be the best way to achieve accountability, the truth and justice for the murder, pain and suffering, and devastation inflicted on us from the worst terrorist attack the world had ever witnessed. I was appalled to learn some of the nineteen al Qaeda operatives were in America for nearly two years before the attacks. I was sickened to learn they were met by handlers and had a support network in place to assist them in finding housing, renting cars, and helping them with their flying lessons. I was horrified to learn they rented small aircraft and flew up and down the East River in New York City, as well as around our nation's capital, seeking out their targets. 9/11 did not "just happen"; it was a highly sophisticated plot that took years to plan and money to support it. The attacks were carried out by nineteen terrorists who barely spoke English and had never visited or lived in our country before, so how were they able to travel to America and carry out their murderous reign of terror?

Holding the financiers and those who aided and abetted the nineteen terrorists accountable for the murder of nearly 3,000 innocent men, women, and children and the pain and suffering inflicted on the survivors and those left behind has been a focus of mine and numerous other 9/11 victims' family members and survivors for over a decade.

Americans and the world deserve answers. We deserve to know the truth. Our national security depends on an informed public, military, and Congress in order to protect us. I have worked for over four years with members of both chambers of Congress, on both sides of the aisle to enact counter-terrorism legislation to deter future catastrophic terrorist attacks on U.S. soil and support resolutions to declassify pertinent documents, including the infamous "redacted 28 pages" kept secret from the American people regarding the intelligence gathering events before and after 9/11.

This is not where my grief story ends. I have stumbled along the way, but I have never stopped trying to do the best I can and to be the best mother to my children. I have spoken at numerous press conferences in Washington, D.C., and given interviews to over thirty news organizations, both domestically and internationally. I presented an inspirational speech at Carnegie Hall – speaking to youth about choosing a positive path after a horrible experience and to not allow hatred from a violent criminal act control your life. I have spoken at a memorial for family members after their loss from a downed Russian aircraft by terrorists, offering condolences, strength, and unity in our shared grief, and I have spoken at the National Press Club in Washington, D.C., addressing President El Sisi of Egypt's delegation on the merits of counter-intelligence legislation. All of these experiences have helped me turn my grief into something positive.

What drives me to push for transparency, enact counter-terrorist legislation to deter future terrorist attacks, and shed a light on the continued threat we face today, is my three children. They are my pride, my joy, and my life. Growing up in a post 9/11 world has not been easy and I would do anything to make it better. We all deserve a safer country and a safer world from the nonstop threat of radical Islamic terrorism.

Since 9/11, I have truly seen the worst and the best of mankind. Our country was united in grief, and we remained strong. People from all over the world reached out to our broken families. The Saint James 9/11 Bereavement Group, Pam, and her wonderful volunteers were a godsend. A lot of healing went on in our weekly meetings, where we cried, sang, learned, mourned, and remembered our loved ones.

Whatever path or journey your life is on, whatever obstacle you are faced with, I wish you peace, love, and happiness always. Time does not heal all wounds, but it certainly helps. When life becomes overwhelming, give yourself a break and remember to take care of yourself. We never "get over" our loss; it takes hard work and determination to learn how to live with it. I have been blessed in many ways, and I have learned happiness is a choice. I hope happiness is a part of your life, and if it is not, you will be able to make that choice some day, too.

A Note from Pam: *I am pleased to share that Terry became "National Chairperson of the 9/11 Families & Survivors United for Justice Against Terrorism." On July 15, 2016, after many years of tedious hours of teamwork to urge President Obama to release "The 28 Pages," he approved them for release, and later the "28 pages" were released to the American people. On September 28, 2016, "JASTA-S. 240" became law.*

On the fifteenth anniversary of September 11, 2001, Terry and her family received the "Tree of Life Award" from The Saint James 9/11 Bereavement Support Group.

Congratulations for commendable transformative grief in action, Strada Family!

RONALD T.

(The setting is at the site of their new home, under construction at the time, in Far Hills, New Jersey.)

"A life well lived." Ron lived without fear, without excuses, and without regrets. He had a life filled with many joys. Why are we here today? Two months ago, Ron told me he did not want an elaborate funeral or burial. He wanted to be cremated and his ashes scattered about. I told him I would take him on a sailboat ride because I knew that he loved sailing. He said he just wanted his friends to have a big party at this house. Right now I really don't feel like having a party, but I do thank all of you for coming today. I think Ron was envisioning the house slightly differently, but we can never be sure what the future holds. When I think of Ron, I think of love. Ron was love. Nothing pleased him more than just being with his family.

Ron was everything that was good on this earth. He was conscientious, honest, generous, patient, consistent, persistent, hardworking, reliable, funny, confident, good-natured, and more. Ron was comfortable in his own skin. Ron was happy. If Ron wasn't at work, he was with us. We always had fun together, be it at Disney World, the ski slopes, a hike in the woods, the trips to the park, circus, zoo, or the beach, weekend bike rides, reading books, washing the cars, and playing the piano so the kids could dance. We were always together. On Saturdays, we had "family fun night" when we would play Ring around the Rosie, Duck-Duck-Goose, Leap Frog, or Do the Can-Can. He was always there for us. Our kids anxiously awaited each annual ritual like going to see the fireworks, the balloon festival, the air show, going to the farm to pick pumpkins, or chopping down our Christmas tree.

Fourteen years ago I started giving Ron haircuts when I found out he gave a $15 tip for a $10 haircut. I had been trying to get him to go back to the barber, but he said he just didn't want to waste the time.

Through his quiet gentle ways, he taught me how to live my life better. Learn from the past, live for today, have no fears or regrets, look hopefully toward the future. Ron was the happiest person I had ever met. His personality was so even-keeled that sometimes it was hard to discern his mood. He really seemed not disturbed by things that were out of his control. He would come home from work and I would say "How are you doing?" and he would say "Good." I'd say "I heard the market was down five hundred points today." He'd say, "Yeah, it was." But there was no mistaking his jubilation the day we got married and the days when each of our three children had been born. You could see his heart grow with each child. When Alana was born, Ron cut the umbilical cord and the doctor handed her to him. The two of them just stared at each other. Then Ron got our camera and took pictures of her in his arms. He spent many hours marveling at her.

Danielle brought out more of Ron's playful side, as she always likes to have fun and be silly. While I was pregnant with Andrew, Ron who was generally a very private person, he took ultrasound pictures to the office and asked the co-workers if they wanted to see the pictures of his son. The two of them were inseparable. The void in their lives from this loss is almost, too much for me to bear. It doesn't matter how good a mother I am, I cannot be their father. Ron used to hold them while skiing down the mountain when they were a year old. When they were a year, he put them on skis; when they were three years old, he took them for a helicopter ride. He always did things that thrilled them.

The most important thing to Ron was his family. He always made me feel comfortable and secure. Ron and I were together for more than fourteen years during which I faced many difficult moments. He stayed by my side through my ups and downs and never once wavered. I knew he would always be there for me. I think Ron and I grew to be better people for having known each other.

On 9/11, that Tuesday started out like any other Tuesday. Ron got up, got ready for work, and gave me a back rub and a kiss goodbye. I consider myself very blessed for having been loved by him.

"PLEASE TEACH PEACE, RESPECT, AND UNDERSTANDING."

A Note from Pam: *Karen, I can't help but think that Ron was very blessed for having been loved by you! So happy you finally made it to our group. Karen donates her time aiding the 9/11 Memorial Mass of Remembrance and has hosted in the past lovely gatherings for our 9/11 groups at her beautiful home. She has done an outstanding job as a mother. Ron's great gifts poured out from the hearts of you, and your beautiful children, will make this world a better place.*

Chapter 32

The Rippling Effects on Those Who Reached Out

Just as the ripples spread out when a single pebble is dropped into the water, the actions of Individuals can have far-reaching effects.
Dalai Lama

I n this final chapter, we learn about one of the volunteers who reached out to these families over an extended period of time. The rippling effects of the 9/11 attacks extended from The Saint James 9/11 Bereavement Support Group families into the lives of our volunteers, friends, families, and people in our community who were connected to our group. Patricia is just one of several volunteers who continues to lend a hand today to the programs and foundations started by our families.

REFLECTIONS FROM PATRICIA GILBRETH, VOLUNTEER

All my life I have always found great satisfaction in helping others, knowing that I often receive as much as those I assist. Thinking back now to the days, weeks, and months following the horrific events of 9/11, I knew I had to do whatever I could to hopefully make life a bit easier for those suffering such unimaginable losses. In putting my thoughts to paper and recalling all emotions of that time, I realize my actions were a catalyst to continue increasing my efforts to help others.

In September 2001, my good friend, Ginger and I came to Saint James each week to serve as caregivers to the children brought to the bereavement group meetings. We were humbled to help in this small way and enjoyed being with the children, whose innocent lives were forever changed. I will never forget feeling the pain that I observed, pain that was so very palpable in the meeting room, as we passed each day to go to the childcare area. The grief-stricken and shocked faces there told of each person's personal loss. I remember thinking how wonderful the facilitators were in providing support, love, understanding, and compassion with the meaningful activities that were planned, certainly not an easy task considering the circumstances. However, as each week passed, I did observe a gradual lightening of the group's mood. I even managed a smile when I noticed brighter faces and heard light laughter.

I was sorry when my time at the group ended as the meetings became less frequent. My involvement did continue though through my special friendship that has grown over the years with the Hannaford family, starting in September of 2001. I did not know Eileen and her boys on 9/11, but offered them support then just as I continue to do so now. Being involved with them personally and through my work for *The Kevin J. Hannaford, Sr. Foundation* has enriched my life immensely. I also reach out and support a group called "Heartworks", an amazing group that stemmed directly from our bereavement group by one of the member's sisters, Megan McDowell, who is a social worker and was mentioned earlier in this book. Her outreach to others is commendable.

I continue to help with the 9/11 Memorial Mass of Remembrance at the Shrine each year. I am honored to be there as a volunteer of the bereavement group. I am always encouraged in seeing how "our" families have continued living positively to honor their lost loved ones. I will continue to think back on those days at the bereavement group with mixed emotions and with a sense of fulfillment that I participated in something so special, but also with sadness for the reason we were all brought together.

A Hope-Filled Blessing

Although our world is full of suffering... it is full also of the overcoming of it. My wish for you is that all your days of sadness and sorrow will be met with care and will germinate into the seeds that grow compassion.
Helen Keller

The pain and sorrow will never be forgotten, for the grief still lingers on in all our suitcases. The families of The Saint James 9/11 Bereavement Support Group journeyed forward, into an altered life far from that which they had once assumed filled with many hopes and dreams. Thus, they have grown stronger from their broken places. They have become wiser, braver, and more compassionate. They have worked hard and have made good choices. They will continue the message of goodness and the love they were given. It is the seeds planted in their hearts during their difficult and dark days that will scatter, lending hope to places in our fractured world and leading them to pay it forward one person at a time. My wish for them is that they become a catching force and a sympathetic, as well as an empathetic influence for those suffering in grief. These 9/11 families through my eyes have transformed into the "People of Hope."

After two years of sixty-eight sessions and more than three hundred hours, for me, our time together was a religious experience. I witnessed God's manifestation and great wish for the bereaved of

9/11. Over flowing blessings of dignity, respect and honor, enfolded in a loving and compassionate manner around Gods' hurting 9/11 families opening a door to transfiguration and transformation. My heart beams with gladness. All our hearts will forever be entwined. I end this story extending a warm blessing over you, The Saint James 9/11 Bereavement Support Group, so too, I share the blessing over all 9/11 families everywhere.

I pray this blessing over you with the golden word "Peace" in the forefront of my mind.

God on High, hear my prayer, rise up the Survivor Families of 9/11.
Send forth Your blessings, God of hopefulness,
gently and abundantly over them.
God of Peace, be near them on their journey forward.
God of Light, go before them to illuminate their path ahead.
God of Protection and Mercy, stay beside
them always with your loving Care.
God of Wisdom, stand behind them to guide them
in times when they don't understand.
God of Love, abide within their hearts that others
might hear the sound of their beats.
Set them free, Oh God, to fly like eagles over the
parched earth blocking out the darkness and Ushering
in Your Divine Goodness and Light. AMEN

P.S. Set me as a seal upon your hearts.
(Sol. 8:6)

Lovingly,
PAM KOCH

Thank You

So many people reached out to us and it has been so many
years that I would be remiss to start to begin to list them
all for fear I could miss one. Please know that it is with
deep gratefulness in our hearts we thank you for
Lighting, Our path
With comfort and hope.

✦ Editors ✦

I am Most Grateful
~To~
Kara Starcher of starcherdesigns.com ~ Chloe, West Virginia
William Summers of The Summers Group ~
Basking Ridge, New Jersey

~Proofreaders~

Christine Perrault ~ Mashpee, Massachusetts
Regina Townsend ~ North Chatham, Massachusetts
~And ~
About the Author ~Kerry Gilrane ~ Fort Mill, South Carolina

You were all invaluable to me!

Dedications

This book is dedicated to the victims of 9/11. I will lift up my eyes to you, high into the heavens. I vow that your deaths were not in vain. You will live on, just in another way. Your fragrance and honor will be spread into the darkest corners of life and will bloom like the lilies of the fields. I give you a solemn promise that no one can steal: we will never let anyone forget you. Your goodness shall prevail.

"NO DAY SHALL ERASE YOU FROM THE MEMORY OF TIME."
Virgil

This book is dedicated to you, the members of The Saint James 9/11 Bereavement Support Group. You have toiled hard, and you have well earned this dedication for your tenacity, your endurance, your constant commitment to the grief process, and your remarkable dedication to the welfare of your families. Your transformative grief in action has been commendable. You are truly an example of heroism, and you are outstanding Americans who have planted your seeds of compassion. Your goodness has flowed over into the world. You have made a difference for others. It would be an honor and a privilege to have you pass through anyone's path in life, especially mine. I count myself as doubly blessed for knowing you and your mending hearts.

This book is dedicated to my beloved sister, Joan Bundschuh DeVita, 2/15/45 – 3/5/78. Joan, it was your life and death that inspired me to embark into the field of hospice work. Your young life, though gone too soon, has made a difference in this world for others. You are so loved into eternity, Joan.

My darling Bob, you are the love of my life, my rock, and the greatest "pontiff" (bridge builder) I know! Our lives will be forever entwined. You have created a life with me that I never could have imagined. It certainly has been a moving experience. It is a delight for me to be yours. You fill my life with the blessing of you each and every day. Your gentle and kind, loving, and patient spirit is the gift you are. I dedicate this book to you, with much love in my heart, with everlasting thanksgiving to the God who chose you for me. My love for you is timeless, my darling and loving Bobby.

To Michael Clark, a stranger I have never met, but with whom I have the common link of stem cells. You are truly among the "People of the Wings" in every way as I learned you were in the Air Force at the time of transplant. Michael, your unselfish and unconditional act of becoming a donor has made this book "happen" and has given me almost fifteen years of new life. I will always be deeply grateful to you for your heroic deed. As a result, you have bestowed on me blessings beyond compare of building memories with others to love, most especially meeting and knowing six beautiful grandchildren who fill my life with wonder and joy. Thank you, always and forever, for the most sacred gift of life itself. A profound appreciation beats in my heart for you each and every day.

Pam Koch

Acknowledgements

To my mother and father for your loving support and example of Christian witness. May your souls rest in peace, and until we meet again, may God hold you in the palm of His hands. Filled with a loving and grateful heart for you always.

Pam

To you, my cherished and adored children, Kerry, Jessica, Rob, and Tim, for you are all I live for and everything I need. It is you of whom I am well pleased. You are my reason for being, my purpose for living. I fought cancer with all my might for you. You are my inspiration. You have touched the world with your goodness and love and have made the world a better place for those around you. You were the lighthouses for me in my darkest of days. Celebrate life, love tenderly, create memories, and strive only to make the best of your days, never to take those days for granted. Your life is sacred and has meaning. You are the artwork of Him who created you. May respect and honor be yours as in turn that you may do unto others in this same manner. Always remember that what you are creating is a life of legacy. Your example is everything for those who come after you. Commitment, along with principals, virtues, and morals, are not just words to be taken lightly, but are the telling truths of whom you truly are. Think about them then adapt them into the forefront of your lives as you journey forward, for you shall not pass this way again. Pass them on to others that they might know God through you. I pray you keep sending your beacon of light, brilliantly upon all those to see. Wherever I go, you go with me, forever in my heart, and loving you always for all time and into eternity.

Mom

My most glorious hallelujah moments came on the announcement of your births, my grandchildren Grace, Lucy, Sean, Avery, Will, and Quincy. I could never forget you, you whom I love so much. Your faces bring euphoria to my soul. Your presence sends my spirit soaring. You are the sweetest blessings of my life, Sugar Lambs. I have carved your names into the tablets of my heart forever. You bring me great joy and happiness all the days of my life. With you, every day is Christmas! Always remember the secret code! And may the force be with you!! I love each and every one of you with all my heart and soul. Please know I will love you forever and ever and give glory to the Almighty God for creating you for me to adore.

Lambie

To you, Monsignor John Carroll, Father Patrick O'Donovan, Monsignor William Capik, Father Peter Krebs, Rev. David Dutcher, Sister Catherine Morrisatt, and in memory of Monsignor Ronald Amandolare, along with the many clergy and denominations throughout Basking Ridge and the surrounding areas, your prayers were heard. Be assured that your acts of anointing, healing masses, and many prayers prayed in my name, truly gave me the spiritual strength to go forward when I thought there was nothing left in me. Your intercessions made miracles happen in His name.

Pam Koch

To the many doctors and nurses who worked gallantly to enable me to fight for my life. Most especially I praise the heads of my medical teams: Dr. Daniel Moriarty, MD, medical oncology, Overlook Hospital,

Summit, New Jersey; Dr. Roger Strair, MD, PhD, hematology and oncology, Robert Wood Johnson University Hospital, New Brunswick, New Jersey; Dr. Ann Jakubowski, MD, hematology and oncology, along with the transplant team at Memorial Sloan Kettering Cancer Center.

These doctors worked tirelessly to save lives for leukemia and blood cancer patients within the walls of great institutions. Respectful and heartfelt appreciation flows through my veins literally because of you. Your knowledge, wisdom, and skills have tied the bow on the greatest gift of all: "new life."

Survivor Pam Koch

A special thank you to my compassionate niece, Dr. Cherry Estilo-Fitzpatrick, DMD, Memorial Sloan Kettering Cancer Center for your loving spirit and support, many visits, and healing touch. I am so proud to call you family.

Aunt Pam

To my many nurses and most especially Kerry Gilrane, Molly Sullivan Maurer, Karen Witt, Virginia Moriarty, Nancy Pain, Lauren Oelkers you gave generously your compassion, comfort, and expertise. It is with an indebted heart I will sing your praises.

Pam

To all our supportive family members, whose names could fill a second book, along with our many friends most especially Prudence and Terry Pigott, and the Delbarton Mothers Guild and tennis team who stood alongside us during those difficult days, please know a fragrant bouquet of gratitude, love, and thanksgiving our family expresses to you.

Pam

Bibliography

BOOKS

Covey, Stephen, PhD., *The 7 Habits of Highly Effective People*, New York: Simon And Schuster Publishers, 2013. Book Cover

Chopra, Deepak MD. *The Deeper Wound*, New York: Harmony Press Publishers, 2001. Book Cover

Doka, Kenneth J. PhD. *Disenfranchised Grief: Recognizing Hidden Sorrow*, Lexington Kentucky: Lexington Books Publishing, 1989. *Disenfranchised Grief: New Directions, Challenges, and Strategies for Practice*, Champaign, Illinois: expanded edited volume Research Press, 2002. Pg.5

Keller, Helen. *The World I Live In & Optimism: A Collection of Essays*, Mineola, New York: Dover Publications, 2010. Pg.89

Kubler-Ross, Elizabeth, M.D., *Death: The Final Stage of Growth*, New York: MacMillan Publishing Company, 1969. *On Death and Dying 40th edition*, Abingdon, England: Taylor and Francis, 2008. Pg.96

Langshur, Eric and Klemp, Nate, *Start Here: A life long Habit of wellbeing*, New York: Simon and Schuster, 2017.

Rando, Therese, PhD. BCETS, BCBT. *Treatment of Complicated Mourning*, Champaign, Illinois: Research Press, 1993. Pg.393-450

Teresa, Mother. *A Simple Path*, Compiled by Vardey, Lucinda, Ballentine Books a division of Penquin Random House Inc., New York: 1995. Pg. 1

Worden, J. William, PhD. ABPP *Grief Counseling and Grief Therapy*, 4th edition, New York: Springer Publishing Company, 2010. Pg. 84

PRAYER BOOKS / ROMAN RITUAL/BIBLE

The New American Bible, revised edition c 2010, 1991, 1986, 1970
Confraternity of Christian Doctrine, Inc., Washington, DC All
Rights Reserved

The New Union Prayer Book of Awe –A Litany of Remembrance by
Rabbi Sylvan Kamens and Rabbi Jack Reimer taken from Gates of
Repentance: The New Union Prayerbook of Awe, copyright 1998,
revised 1996 by the Central Conference of Reformed Rabbis and
Women of Reform Judaism and are under the copyright protection
of the Central Conference Of American Rabbis and printed by
permission of CCAR. All Rights Reserved

Order of Christian Funerals, Collegeville Minnesota, The Liturgical
Press, 1989

Roman Catholic Daily Missal, Angelus Press 1962

MUSIC

Alexander, Paul LCSW WWW.GRIEFSONG.COM
"Light a Candle"
"Pretty Balloon"
"Song for America"
"Tree of Memory"
"Wrap Myself in a Rainbow"

Groban, Josh ~ WARNER BROTHERS RECORDS
"You Raise Me Up"
"Your Still You"

Halligan, Robert ~ BLATANT PROMOTIONS PRS/MCPS
"Sunshine" Lyrics

VIDEOS

Miller, James E. D. Min. ~ Willowgreen, Inc.
You Shall Not Be Overcome

PROSE
Weed, Susun S. "In the Garden"
WWW.SUSUNWEED.COM

MAGAZINE ARTICLE
Barrett, Jennifer "The Only Place Where I feel Normal" *Newsweek Magazine*

About the Author

 Pamela Koch is a breast-cancer survivor who was called back to work as a pastoral bereavement counselor for the families of 9/11 in the small suburban town of Basking Ridge, New Jersey. Among her long list of abundant gifts in life, Pam adds the gift of time that was given to her that she might marvel at the goodness that sprung from this 9/11 bereavement group at *Saint James Church*. Pam has received numerous awards and distinctions for her contributions to her community, and today she lives with her husband, Bob, in Naples, Florida, and Chatham, Massachusetts, where she creates memories with her children, grandchildren, family, and friends.